THE AGED IN
THE WELFARE STATE

The Interim Report of a Survey of Persons
aged 65 and over in Britain, 1962 and 1963

by

PETER TOWNSEND
Department of Sociology, University of Essex

and

DOROTHY WEDDERBURN
Department of Applied Economics, University of Cambridge

assisted by SYLVIA KORTE and SHEILA BENSON
(University of Essex)

Occasional Papers on Social Administration No. 14
(Editorial Committee under the Chairmanship of
Professor R. M. Titmuss)

Published by
G. Bell & Sons Ltd.,
York House, Portugal Street, London, W.C.2.

First Published July 1965
Second Edition 1966
Third Edition 1970

© *1965 by the Social Administration*
Research Trust.

ISBN 07135 0956 2

Printed in England by
The Chapel River Press, Andover, Hants.

FOREWORD

This series of *Occasional Papers* was started in 1960 to supply the need for a medium of publication for studies in the field of social policy and administration which fell between the two extremes of the short article and the full-length book. It was thought that such a series would not only meet a need among research workers and writers concerned with contemporary social issues, but would also strengthen the links between students of the subject and administrators, social workers, committee members and others with responsibilities and interests in the social services.

Most of the papers in this series have been written by members of the Department of Social Science and Administration at the London School of Economics and Political Science. Contributions are, however, welcome from workers in other universities and institutions and should be submitted to the Editorial Committee. A complete list of earlier papers in this series is printed on the back of this volume.

Richard M. Titmuss

Contents

Preface to the 1970 Edition

Since this preliminary report was published in 1965 and reprinted in 1966, the major report on the survey of old people in the United States and Denmark as well as in Britain, which is referred to on pp. 6 and 7, has been published (*Old People in Three Industrial Societies* by Ethel Shanas, Peter Townsend, Dorothy Wedderburn, Henning Friis, Paul Milhøj, and Jan Stehouwer, London, Routledge & Kegan Paul, 1968). However, *The Aged in the Welfare State* has not in any sense been replaced by the later book. It contains material of specific relevance to the aged in Britain and to social policy which is not published elsewhere. Moreover, although there have been changes in services since 1965 (in particular, increases in rates of benefit) the relative situation of the aged in society has not been substantially affected. The findings can be regarded as offering a truthful picture of the conditions and circumstances of old people in Britain today. Later research, particularly the report by the Ministry of Pensions on *The Financial and Other Circumstances of Retirement Pensioners* (London, HMSO, 1966) has tended to reinforce the picture presented here of the general scale and nature of need.

December, 1969

Preface

The survey described in these pages forms part of a cross-national survey of old people aged 65 and over being carried out in the United States, Denmark and Britain. Its organisation, financing and history are rather unusual and should be briefly explained. It originated in a series of meetings of the European Social Science Research Committee of the International Association of Gerontology, of which Professor Richard Titmuss was then chairman, during the years 1956–1959,[1] and a small pilot study for a cross-national survey was carried out in England in 1959.[2] The principal object of the proposed survey was to measure the extent of disability or incapacity among the aged in relation to their family and social relationships, occupations, housing and levels of income. It seemed that the time had come to put a series of local studies into perspective, take advantage of the definitions and hypotheses that had already been advanced and build up a more systematic body of knowledge in national and international terms about ageing and the aged.

Eventually, social scientists in the three countries were able to concert their plans and in 1961 they were fortunate to find a body able and willing to finance, on the heavy scale required, their collaborative venture. We wish to express our thanks to the National Institute of Mental Health of the Public Health Service of the United States.[3] The study was based on a double strategy. The research workers in the three countries accepted precisely comparable methods of procedure and research. They agreed on a common questionnaire covering health, family and social activities, income, occupation and retirement, and adopted similar definitions and coding frames. National probability samples of persons aged 65 and over were drawn in each country and interviewing carried out according to agreed instructions during the same period of 1962 (April to July).

By late 1964, the research workers had met on twelve occasions, both in the United States and Europe, to co-ordinate plans. Care was taken to see that the technical execution of the survey was as closely comparable as, at this stage in the evolution of the social sciences, it seemed possible to achieve. Even the response rates (84 per cent in

---

1. See Friis, H., "Cross-National Research on Old Age", *International Social Science Journal*, XV, No. 3, 1963, pp. 451–455; Shanas, E., "Some Observations on Cross-National Surveys of Ageing", *The Gerontologist*, March, 1963; and *Cross-National Surveys of Old Age*, published by the Division of Gerontology, University of Michigan, Ann Arbor, Michigan, 1958.

2. Townsend, P., and Rees, B., *The Personal, Family and Social Circumstances of Old People: Report of an Investigation carried out in England to Pilot a Future Cross-National Survey*, London, London School of Economics, 1959.

3. The grant designation was MH-05511. Later the Division of Community Health Services continued to finance the project on a generous scale (CH-00053).

Denmark, 86 per cent in Britain and 89 per cent in the United States) were, in the event, similar. A cross-national report is now being prepared.

But although the cross-national research was given priority, another strategy was adopted—of supplementing it with some national research. In each country there were interests, services or conditions which demanded special attention. In the United States, for example, it was desirable to include questions about methods of financing payment for medical care, a matter of major importance and debate in that country. In Britain, the interest was in the old people's experiences of the health and welfare services, the development of which was being anxiously discussed.

On the other hand, in both Britain and the United States it seemed unnecessary to collect more than essential data on income because a considerable amount of information was already being or was about to be produced by the government in the United States and by independent research workers in Britain. Yet in Denmark there was an urgent need for the collection of such financial information on a full scale.

The research workers in each of the three countries therefore added national questions to the basic cross-national questionnaire and agreed that the national reports as well as a cross-national report might be prepared and published. The Danes also decided to interview persons aged 62–64 as well as persons aged 65 and over, and in Britain a more complex pattern of follow-up studies was developed. Because of the importance attached to the circumstances and problems of minorities among the elderly population—such as those who are bedfast or otherwise severely incapacitated, those who are socially isolated, those who are receiving certain welfare services and those who have very recently retired—it was decided, first, to draw another random sample of the population aged 65 and over and carry out a second stage of interviews in the autumn of 1962—to bring the numbers about whom there was full information to over 4,000. This had the further advantages of furnishing a check on the representativeness of some figures from the first sample and of obtaining information at a different season of the year.

It was decided, second, to obtain information for those persons aged 65 and over who were living in institutions. Although fewer than 5 per cent of the elderly live in institutions, they have certain pronounced characteristics and it is difficult to generalise confidently about the processes of ageing and the conditions of the aged without taking them into account. We therefore drew a special sample of hospitals, nursing Homes and residential Homes and sought to obtain information for up to 2,500 persons aged 65 and over—half of whom we proposed to interview. Inevitably difficulties were encountered in carrying out this research. A special team of interviewers had to be recruited and trained and consultations with those in administrative charge of the institutions were necessary to guarantee confidentiality and respect for the feelings of those who were ill and infirm. The survey was carried out in February–July 1963 and information was obtained for 2,205 elderly persons.

Finally it was decided to carry out a special follow-up inquiry of those old people who were found to be socially isolated and housebound. It had been hoped to interview a sub-sample of the 4,000 interviewed in private households throughout Britain in 1962, but this unfortunately proved impossible. Instead, four contrasting areas— Harrow, Northampton, Oldham and a rural part of Norfolk—were visited and a sample of elderly persons selected in each area. Over 500 old people were interviewed briefly in a 'screening' operation designed to identify the isolated, the lonely and the housebound, and 200 of these were interviewed at length.

The work in Britain began in late 1961, much of it based on the London School of Economics of the University of London, but with the active help of the Department of Applied Economics of the University of Cambridge. The final stages of the analysis are being carried out at the new University of Essex. Dorothy Wedderburn, Senior Research Officer of the Department at Cambridge, and Peter Townsend, formerly lecturer in Social Administration at the London School of Economics and now Professor of Sociology at the University of Essex, have jointly directed the survey of the elderly in private households, and Peter Townsend has been director of the project as a whole. Mrs Caroline Woodroffe and Miss Sheila Benson have played a leading part in the analysis of the survey of institutions; Miss Sylvia Korte has been responsible for a large part of the analysis of the private household survey and has contributed much of value to these pages; and Mr Jeremy Tunstall is in charge of the follow-up survey of the isolated and lonely.

This complex of studies could not have been undertaken without the agreement and help of many different people. First and foremost is the Government Social Survey. There is no university or other independent survey organisation in Britain, apart from the market research organisations, which is capable of handling such a major survey, and the Government Social Survey agreed to undertake all the interviewing of 4,000 persons in the two stages of the national survey of the elderly in private households. The director, Mr Louis Moss, and his staff were remarkably tolerant of an investigation whose complexity was not fully apparent to any of the participants at the beginning. It should not be supposed that their contribution was confined to operating a plan which others had developed. From the start the staff of the Social Survey, and particularly Miss Amelia Harris and Mrs Myra Woolf, played a leading role in helping to work out the questionnaires, definitions of concepts, organisation of field-work and programme of analysis. They also gave valuable comments about our interpretation of the material, and Appendix 2 was compiled with the generous assistance of Mr Ronald Blunden. We were most fortunate in having such help.

We must also thank the government for making the work possible. Permission had to be sought before we could use the services of the

Social Survey and, as is usual in these matters, this depended to some extent on the support of the principal government representatives of the subjects under study (in this case the Ministers of Health, Housing and Local Government, and Labour, the Minister of Pensions and the Chairman of the National Assistance Board). Moreover, the permission of the Ministry of Health and of the Scottish Home and Health Department to enter National Health Service hospitals also had to be sought. Permission was generously granted and we only hope that the results, some of which are reported in the following pages, will be held to justify the time and trouble taken by many people to draw what must always be a fine line between the responsibilities of government and those of independent research. We must emphasise, of course, that none of these bodies, nor the individuals who have been personally involved, is responsible for the conclusions we have drawn from the data.

We must thank the Regional Hospital Boards, County Councils and County Borough Councils, voluntary associations and private proprietors for permission to enter their premises. At various stages we have received valuable help in analysing our data from the Hampstead Tabulating Centre and, latterly, from the Computer Unit of the University of London. Many individuals have contributed to the work. Apart from those already mentioned we must acknowledge the help of Brian Rees, Royston Lambert, Gay Boehm, Jan Ameen (formerly Walker), Gurmukh Singh, Alan Stuart, Daphne Partos and David Skilton. Valuable comments on earlier drafts were made by officials of the Ministries of Pensions, Health, Housing and Labour, the National Assistance Board and the Board of Inland Revenue. We should also like to thank Brian Abel-Smith, Tony Lynes, Jeremy Tunstall, J. L. Nicholson, Brian Reddaway and Adrian Sinfield for similar help.

Finally, we must explain that this is a preliminary report. It does not cover all the subject-matter of the survey. The preparation of the results from a major survey—particularly one which forms part of an experimental cross-national study—necessarily takes time. We have produced this interim report because it seems important to publish as soon as possible the information which is particularly relevant for immediate policy decisions. This has determined the selection of subject-matter presented in this report.

Introduction

Between 1901 and 1947 the numbers of persons in Britain who were aged 65 and over grew from under two to five millions. Yet in that period very little information on the problems of the aged living at home or receiving treatment and care in hospitals and other institutions was published. It is an extraordinary fact. At the turn of the century there had been a few studies on pensions and the effect of the Poor Law, three of them by Charles Booth.[1] In 1909 the reports of the Majority and Minority of the Royal Commisson on the Poor Laws appeared, and they both contained sections on the aged.[2] In later years there were short passages on the problems of old age in various reports of general surveys.[3] Otherwise there was a dearth of published information and, apparently, of interest too.

Suddenly, in the late forties and fifties, or so it may seem to the historian of the written and spoken word, the problems of old age were discovered. The Nuffield Foundation pioneered the financing of a few studies, including the remarkable work of J. H. Sheldon.[4] The trickle of carefully documented studies became a modest stream, slightly preceding the floodwaters of interest and research in the subject which were released in the United States in the mid-1950s. Among some of the influential studies in Britain have been those of Dr Alex Comfort on the biology of senescence,[5] Dr Alan Welford and his colleagues on psychological adjustment in old age,[6] and Mr F. Le Gros Clark on ageing in industry.[7] There have been many sociological socio-medical and socio-economic surveys which have been based on interviews with samples of the elderly population.[8]

To the sociologist this accumulation of information is a source of encouragement. It is beginning to be possible to put forward hypotheses—about isolation, poverty, adjustment to retirement, the

---

1. Booth, C., *Pauperism: A Picture; and the Endowment of Old Age: An Argument*, London, MacMillan, 1892; *The Aged Poor: Condition*, Londen, MacMillan, 1894; and *Old Age Pensions and the Aged Poor*, London, MacMillan, 1899.
2. *Report of the Royal Commission on the Poor Laws*, Cd. 4499, London, HMSO, 1909.
3. See, for example, Caradog-Jones, D., *The Social Survey of Merseyside*, London, Hodder & Stoughton, 1934; Rowntree, B. S., *Poverty and Progress*, London, Longmans, 1941.
4. Sheldon, J. H., *The Social Medicine of Old Age*, Oxford University Press for the Nuffield Foundation, 1948.
5. Comfort, A., *Ageing: The Biology of Senescence*, London, Routledge & Kegan Paul (revised edition), 1964.
6. Welford, A. T., *Ageing and Human Skill*, London, Oxford University Press for the Nuffield Foundation, 1958.
7. For example, Le Gros Clark, F. and Dunne, A. C., *Ageing in Industry*, London, The Nuffield Foundation, 1955.
8. A selected list is given in Appendix I for readers who may wish to learn more about old people in particular localities or regions.

family, marriage and social welfare—which have implications not only for our understanding of ageing and the aged but human relationships and society in general. The growing body of empirical data is at last making it possible to formulate tentative theories of social change. However, the advances in knowledge should not be exaggerated. Many surveys of old age have been restricted in their geographical scope and their objectives, and have not been designed to show the inter-relationship of social, economic and physical factors. The problems of ageing involve a number of different disciplines and some of them can only be understood in an inter-disciplinary context.

But no-one who is active in social gerontology can feel comfortable in dealing with theoretical questions alone. Questions of policy arise insistently. In recent years the increase in the scale and number of the various social problems of old age seems by any standards to have outstripped the capacities of most industrialised societies for dealing with them. In Britain a substantial amount of legislation enacted between 1944 and 1948 affected the aged. The National Insurance Act of 1946 provided for retirement pensions at higher levels. The National Assistance Act of 1948 reinforced improvements which had been introduced in the war and not only allowed for payments up to, or nearly up to, minimum subsistence standards for old people and others who did not have pensions, or whose pensions were insufficient to pay for rent and other minimum needs, but also laid upon local authorities the duty to provide residential accommodation. The Health Service, Housing and National Assistance Acts included clauses which gave a basis for many important developments in domiciliary services for the aged—such as home help and mobile meals services and the provision of special housing. All this generated a certain complacency. It was widely believed that the legislation had extended and consolidated the social services to such an extent that the new 'welfare state', which had also brought full employment and a more egalitarian tax system, had succeeded in dealing with most of our major social problems.

But slowly information produced by the various studies of the aged, which showed that social provision was not as completely effective as had been supposed, reached the public. Some major problems, such as the relationship between pension levels and both price and wage levels, and the co-ordination of domiciliary and institutional services, had not been anticipated in the post-war legislation. Others had not been met by the welfare 'system' that resulted. Many services, such as geriatric nursing and housing, were shown to have serious shortcomings or deficiencies. Public sympathy for the aged was aroused. Yet sufficient information for understanding the problems and as a basis for effective policy was still lacking. Previous studies were limited in scope and depth. Certain general questions remained to be answered. Just how effective was the existing range of social services in meeting the needs of the elderly? Could it be shown, as some alleged, that the collective provision of such services was having undesirable secondary effects in undermining family responsibility or individual self-respect? How far could it be said that the 'needs' of the elderly as they were identified in 1944 and the following years were not met, or could now better be met, by private provisions; or in other words, how far could it be said that advances in prosperity made it possible for society to wind up some of the social services just as patients who were learning to walk again could at some point throw away their crutches?[1] Or how far, as others maintained, were new and in some ways more complex needs developing as a result of social change? And were social services not only an integral but an increasingly important part of any complex society which depended on efficient organisation and rapid economic growth?[2]

Although this inquiry was part of a comparative study in three countries which had differing social structures and historical developments, and whose primary object was to contribute to the theoretical understanding of the social problems of ageing, one of its subsidiary objects at a national level was to give some at least of the facts which might restrict the area of controversy on these matters and show the scope of future action. We were concerned to obtain evidence on a comprehensive scale to find how effective the present social services were in meeting the needs of the aged; to find whether it is true that certain functions formerly performed by the family have been taken over by the social services; to examine how far *new* needs are arising, in the sense that through various forms of education and information people have become dissatisfied with inadequate amateur methods of dealing with certain problems (such as unskilled medical or nursing care at home) and have begun to demand expert professional help of a kind which the family has never been able to supply; and, finally, to get some idea of the extent to which the future needs of the elderly were likely to be affected by changing population and family structure, new forms of housing and rising standards of living.

Methods of research

We decided to collect information from persons aged 65 and over on the relationship between individual disability or incapacity and (i) family and social activities, (ii) occupations, (iii) housing and (iv) levels of income. Two separate samples of persons living throughout Great Britain were selected at random. The first sample was

1. Seldon, A., *Pensions for Prosperity*. Hobart Papers No. 4, London, Institute for Economic Affairs, 1959. For general statements of parts of this theory see De Jouvenal, B., *The Ethics of Redistribution*, 1951; Peacock, A., *The Welfare Society*, Unservile State Papers, No. 2, Liberal Publications Department, 1960; Howe, G., "Reform of the Social Services", in Howell, D. and Raison, T., (eds.), *Principles in Practice*, Conservative Political Centre (for the Bow Group), 1961; Clark, C., *Welfare and Taxation*, Oxford, Catholic Social Guild, 1954; Powell, E., "The Social Services", *The Spectator*, 12th June, 1964; and Goldman, P., in *The Future of the Welfare State*, London, Conservative Political Centre, 1958.
2. Titmuss, R. M., "The Welfare State: Images and Realities", *The Social Science Review*, Vol. XXXVII, No. 1, March, 1963. An excellent example of the necessary inter-relationship of social services and other social institutions is provided by Brian Abel-Smith in his account of the creation of a social security system in the early part of the century from the conflicts of interest and relations between the Friendly Societies, private insurance, the medical profession and the middle and working classes: "Social Security" in Ginsberg, M. (ed.), *Law and Opinion in England in the Twentieth Century*, London, Stevens, 1959. For general discussion of matters relevant to this view, see Titmuss, R. M., *Essays on the Welfare State*, London, Allen and Unwin, 1958 (especially chapter 2); Townsend, P., "Freedom and Equality", *New Statesman*, 14th April, 1961; and Wedderburn, D., "Facts and Theories of the Welfare State" in Saville, J. and Miliband, R. (eds.), *Socialist Register 1965*, London, Merlin Press, 1965.

interviewed from mid-May to July 1962 and the second in November and December of 1962. A questionnaire which on average took just an hour to complete was drawn up and it was extensively piloted in early 1962. A three stage sampling design was employed. The first stage was composed of administrative areas stratified by region and economic status.[1] Eighty such areas were selected with a probability proportionate to their size. Within these eighty areas, a sample of dwelling units was drawn using the electoral register as the sampling frame. Approximately two of every three addresses did not contain elderly people and interviewers rejected these addresses from the samples as soon as they established that no-one aged 65 years and over was living there.

Table A shows the response from individuals who were eligible for interview. It will be seen that 4,067 persons, or nearly 84 per cent of the sample, gave full interviews (or 86 per cent if proxies are included).

TABLE A

Percentage of the sample who were interviewed, 1962

	Number	%
Full interviews	4,067	83·6
Part interviews	26	0·5
Proxy interviews	116	2·4
Refusals	550	11·3
No contact	110	2·2
Total	4,869	100·0

Interviewers were instructed to seek a proxy only when it was clear that an old person was incapable of ever giving an interview, being either too ill or too mentally confused to do so. Interviewers were asked to take great care to establish that the illness from which the old person was suffering was not of a temporary nature. In such instances, the individual responsible for looking after the old person was interviewed as a proxy. Interviews were conducted with 73 proxies in the first stage of interviewing and with 43 proxies in the second stage, representing 2·4 per cent and 2·3 per cent respectively of the sample of old people drawn in each stage. There are considerable difficulties in choosing when to interview proxies. For example, in the first stage, proxies were eventually interviewed for 13 informants, who were originally adjudged to be 'temporarily sick'; it may be that interviewers or their informants simply underestimated the severity of the original illness in these cases.

The state of health of persons upon whose behalf proxies gave an interview was markedly different from that of persons interviewed directly. The former included a large proportion of bedfast and incapacitated persons. They also included a large proportion living

---

1. See Gray, P. G., Corlett, T. and Jones, P., *The Proportion of Jurors as an Index of the Economic Status of a District*, London, Central Office of Information, 1951.

with children and other relatives. We were unable to adjust all our statistical data for the 2·4 per cent upon whose behalf proxy interviews had been carried out, but we adjusted certain parts of the analysis which dealt with mobility and incapacity.[1]

Eleven per cent of those approached for an interview refused (and between a further 3 and 4 per cent refused to answer questions about finance). Many of these elderly persons felt that the subject matter was too personal; others said they were unwell or too busy. More than a quarter of the refusals were made by other members of the household acting on the old person's behalf.

The interviewers did what they could to obtain some information about non-respondents but it was inevitably scrappy. So far as it is possible to say they included a relatively large number of married couples, and of persons of extreme age and infirmity. They also included a relatively large number of persons living in the south-east and midlands and of persons living in areas of high economic status.[2]

When, therefore, the responding sample came to be compared with the elderly population as a whole it was found to include slightly too few people of advanced age, as Table B shows. It also seems that respondents contained relatively large numbers of persons living in the north and north-east and in rural areas. But it must be emphasised that while such differences appeared to exist they were small. In general it may be said that the differences between the responding

TABLE B

Sex and age of the sample of old people and of the elderly population, 1962

	Responding sample		Registrar-General's estimate*	
	Number	%	Number	%
			(000's)	
Sex				
Male	1,674	39·8	2,361	38·4
Female	2,535	60·2	3,790	61·6
Age				
65–69 years	1,457	34·6	2,240	36·4
70–74 years	1,238	29·4	1,711	27·8
75–79 years	848	20·1	1,202	19·6
80–84 years	458	10·9	666	10·8
85+ years	205	4·9	332	5·4
No answer	3	0·1	—	—
Total	4,209	100·0	6,151	100·0

* *Source:* Registrar-General's Quarterly Return for England and Wales. Quarter ended 30th September, 1962. Quarterly Return of the Registrar-General, Scotland. Quarter ended 30th September, 1962

1. Experience suggests that there would be advantages in future surveys in using the same interview schedule for both subjects and proxy respondents (omitting, of course, questions involving attitudes and opinions).
2. The difficulty of obtaining information from non-respondents ruled out even such straightforward exercises as relating their age and marital status to their sex. We cannot in fact say whether differences between non-respondents and respondents shown for one attribute are in fact dependent upon the distribution of another attribute.

sample and the total elderly population are unlikely to affect radically the conclusions of this investigation.[1]

In this report the information from both samples interviewed in 1962 has been amalgamated for simplicity of presentation. The difference between the samples was surprisingly small. For example, 27 per cent of the elderly men in the sample interviewed in the late spring and early summer, compared with 26 per cent interviewed during the winter, were found to be at work, and 9 per cent of women in both samples were at work. Various indices of mobility and health showed little seasonal difference. Ninety-five per cent of the men in both samples were able to get about indoors and outdoors without help. The comparable figures for women were 85 per cent (for the first sample) and 87 per cent (for the second sample). Thirteen per cent of the first sample said they had seen a doctor within the previous week and another 21 per cent within the previous month; the comparable percentages of the second sample were 12 and 20 respectively.

The presentation of the results

The present report does not deal with all the data which the survey has produced. It concentrates upon those matters which have immediate policy implications. The first three chapters in Part I examine the evidence to show how many and what sort of elderly people use the health and welfare services; how far similar services are provided by the family and for how many; and what need there is for expansion in community services for the aged. The chapters in Part II concentrate upon financial provision for the aged, and show the role of the state; the extent to which other sources of income, such as private pensions, savings or the family are important; and, finally, what need there is for further general state financial support or state support directed towards the help of particular groups.

The general conclusions which emerge can be summarised as follows:

(i) there appears to be little evidence to support the view that the social services 'undermine' family responsibility or individual self-respect and self-help (in any meaningful sense of these terms);

(ii) those with the most serious financial problems are single and widowed women; and many of them are among those with the most serious social and welfare problems—those without families;

(iii) community services tend primarily to reach those without, or with comparatively few, family resources;

(iv) national assistance fails to reach all who qualify to receive it;

(v) other social services fail to reach significant numbers of those who need them;

---

1. A full account of methods of inquiry will be given in the forthcoming final report.

(vi) there is also evidence that in social security and in health and welfare the services have been slow to adapt to changing social conditions.

A more detailed summary will be found at the end of this report. The general themes will be explored more fully in later publications. But since decisions are currently being taken about future developments in the social services it seems right to make as much information available as soon as possible. Despite its shortcomings we would hope that the present volume might contribute to an informed discussion about policies for the old in a welfare state.

List of Tables

CHAPTER 1

The Use of the Health and Welfare Services

In Britain there has been a very wide measure of agreement since the war about the desirability of giving more emphasis to community care and less to institutional care in the development of the health and welfare services. The Curtis Report of 1946, followed by the Children Act of 1948, created a new conception of the principles by which children deprived of a normal home life should be treated. The Royal Commission on the Law Relating to Mental Illness of 1954–57 encouraged the spread of active as well as informal methods of treatment and so contributed to the trend towards earlier discharge and the setting up of special services outside the hospital. When the Hospital Plan was published in 1962, the Minister of Health said firmly that its success depended on the 'expected development of the services for prevention and care in the community'.[1] These affected mothers and young children, the mentally disordered and the physically handicapped as well as the aged. The publication subsequently in 1963 of a blue book outlining the plans for the health and welfare services of the local authorities in England and Wales marked the government's recognition of the rapidly increasing importance of these services in social policy.[2]

Similarly, there has been a very wide measure of agreement about the underlying principle of the services for the aged, 'that the best place for old people is their own home, with help from the home services if need be'.[3] This principle has been reaffirmed repeatedly by Government and Opposition spokesmen, as well as by many authorities in medicine and welfare. The real question is whether the principle has been much more than a worthy but largely unfulfilled hope.

During the 1950s no evidence emerged of a pronounced increase in expenditure on domiciliary care, as compared with institutional care, nor of a really marked increase in the scope of home services, with the exception of the home help service.[4] Even in the last few

---

1. *A Hospital Plan for England and Wales*, Cmnd 1604, London, HMSO, January 1962, p. 9.
2. *Health and Welfare: The Development of Community Care*, Cmnd 1973, London, HMSO April 1963.
3. Walker-Smith, Rt. Hon. Derek, in the *Report of the Ninth Conference of the National Old People's Welfare Council*, London, 1958.
4. Townsend, P., *The Last Refuge: A Survey of Residential Institutions and Homes for the Aged in England and Wales*, London, Routledge and Kegan Paul, 1962, pp. 394–400.

years, despite the appearance of significant local authority mental health services, there is still no tangible sign of much greater priority being given to the domiciliary, as compared with the institutional, services, so far as the aged are concerned. For example, the last annual report of the Ministry of Health showed that local authority expenditure in England and Wales on residential accommodation was expected to rise by 39 per cent (from £22·6m. to £31·3m.) between 1961–62 and 1964–65, but by only 32 per cent (from £23·6m. to £31·2m.) for the three local domiciliary services which chiefly help the aged—the home help, home nursing and health visiting services.[1]

But how satisfactory are the health and welfare services for old people in Britain and what strategy should be followed in developing them in the immediate future? The numbers of the elderly in the population, particularly of those aged 80 and over, are continuing to increase. Do we need to expand both the institutional and domiciliary services in proportion, or can we, by enlarging the latter rapidly, limit the increase in the numbers in institutions or actually reduce them? More specifically, should the size of the home help and meals services be tripled or quadrupled? Should vastly more routine medical and other examinations be arranged? Is it time to reorganise completely the administration of local services? These are some of the important practical questions to which our data from the national survey relate.

In this chapter we shall describe the numbers receiving help from the different health and welfare services—hospital, residential, home-help, meals, chiropody, medical and other services—and distinguish how many of them are severely or moderately incapacitated. We shall pay particular attention to the family status and relationships of these persons. In the next chapter we shall consider in more detail the role of the family in relation to the Community Services.

Use of the health and welfare services

We start with the use that is made of the services. In 1963 there were approximately 6·2 million persons aged 65 and over in Great Britain. Rather less than 2 per cent of them (105,000) were in residential Homes, one per cent (60,000) in psychiatric hospitals and nursing Homes, and nearly 2 per cent (115,000) in other hospitals and nursing Homes. Around 4½ per cent, therefore, were in institutions, as Table 1 shows.

The surveys which we undertook in 1962 and 1963 produced information about all categories in Table 1 except the fourth and a small part (probably a third) of the third category. We have assumed that in patterns of disability the old people living in hotels, boarding-houses and so on broadly resemble those living in private households, and old people living in acute general and teaching hospitals and certain special hospitals resemble others living in non-psychiatric hospitals. But of course we would welcome research to check and explore these assumptions.

---

1. *Report of the Ministry of Health for the year ended* 31st *December* 1963, Cmnd 2389, London, HMSO, July 1964.

22

TABLE 1
Estimated number of persons aged 65 and over living in different types of accommodation; Britain, mid-1963

Type of accommodation	Persons aged 65 and over	
	Number	%
1. Residential Homes	105,000	1·7 ⎫
2. Psychiatric hospitals and nursing Homes ...	60,000	1·0 ⎬ 4·5
3. Other hospitals and nursing Homes	115,000	1·8 ⎭
4. Hotels, boarding houses, hostels, common lodging houses, etc.	95,000	1·5 ⎫ 95·5
5. Private households	5,825,000	94·0 ⎭
Total	6,200,000	100·0

Note: The definitions are as used by the Registrar General and the estimates are based on data from the 1961 census, brought up to date from information kindly supplied by the Ministry of Health and the Scottish Home and Health Department.

Large numbers also benefited from other services. During the survey we found that over 4 per cent (258,000) were visited by a home help from the local council (compared with another 9 per cent, or 529,000, who paid ₁or private home help), 1 per cent (66,000) had a meal delivered by the mobile meals service at least once a week, and 7 per cent (423,000) received chiropody treatment through a public or voluntary service (while another 11 per cent, or 660,000, received chiropody treatment privately). Table 2 gives a number of estimates for different services. These estimates are, of course, subject to sampling variation, but official statistics suggest that they are likely to be close to the actual numbers in the population.[1]

Incapacity of persons in institutions and at home

Let us now begin to explore the significance of these figures. Are those who are in institutions or getting services at home really infirm? If not, why must they depend on others? And if they are infirm, why aren't their families looking after them? First, we can compare old people living in institutions with those living at home. Table 3 shows that many more of the former than of the latter are bedfast or housebound, as would be expected.[2] But the table also shows that roughly half the institutional population can walk unaided outside the building. Are these people otherwise handicapped, or could they live at home? If the percentages are converted into absolute numbers we can estimate that of all old people in Britain

1. In 1962 264,725 'elderly and chronic sick cases' were helped by the home help service in England and Wales. Although married couples appear usually to be counted as one case in this total, it also has to be remembered that the number of cases being helped at any particular time of the year is rather smaller. There is a turnover of 'active' cases because of death hospitalisation and other reasons. *Report of the Ministry of Health or the year ended 31st December* 1962, Cmnd 2062, London, HMSO, 1963.
2. The different categories were defined strictly. A person was treated as *bedfast* if he could not get out of bed or a wheelchair and take a few steps without aid; as *confined to the building* if he could get about the building, even for a very short period of the day, on his own feet, but could not walk unaided outside the building even for short distances.

TABLE 2
Estimated number of persons aged 65 and over living in private households who received certain social services; Britain, mid-1963

Social Service	Persons aged 65 and over		
	%	Number in sample	Estimated number in population
Total in private households	100·0	4,067	5,825,000
Home help (local authority)	4·45	181	258,000
Mobile meals (voluntary or local authority)	1·13	46	66,000
Chiropody	7·30	297	423,000
District nurse visiting regularly ...	0·79*	33*	46,000*
Doctor seen in previous week	12·86	523	746,000
Doctor seen in previous month (excluding previous week	20·46	832	1,187,000

Note: * The figure refers only to those defined as permanently bedfast at home. In making estimates we have taken account also of the bedfast among our 'proxy' interviews which covered 116 persons in addition to the 4,067 interviewed. These could not be interviewed and their husbands, wives, children or other relatives supplied some information. Estimated population numbers are subject to sampling error (Appendix 2).

TABLE 3
Mobility of persons aged 65 and over living in institutions and at home; Britain 1962-1963
(samples of 2,205 in institutions and of 4,183 in private households)

Mobility	Institutions	Private households
	%	%
Mobile	32·2	79·8
Mobile outside with difficulty	19·8	7·6
Confined to the building	22·1	10·6
Bedfast	25·9	2·1
Total	100·0	100·0
Number	2,190	4,183

Note: Unclassifiable in the institutional survey, 15

who are bedfast or unable to walk unaided outside the building in which they live, approximately 140,000 are in institutions but approximately 750,000 are in private households.

But a classification according to mobility is only a very rough guide to physical condition. Can we obtain a better overall picture of the incapacities of these populations? A special measure of personal incapacity was developed during the survey, and this was based on whether old people could do six things without aid (walk outdoors, walk indoors, negotiate stairs, wash and bath, dress and cut toenails). This was a simpler version of an index adopted in previous research.[1] If a particular function could not be carried

1. Townsend, P., *op. cit*, Chapter 10 and Appendix 2.

out at all, a score of 2, and if only with difficulty, a score of 1, was given. Each old person was assigned a total score of from 0 to 12 once the scores for the six activities were combined.[1]

Twenty-six per cent of the old people in institutions were bed-fast, compared with 2·1 per cent of those in private households. Another 27 per cent were severely incapacitated (scoring 7 or more on the scale) compared with 7 per cent. But when these figures were related to the total population the more arresting fact emerges that, as Table 4 shows, less than a quarter of the most incapacitated people in the elderly population (i.e. bedfast or otherwise severely incapacitated) are living in institutions. They number just under 150,000 in a total of nearly 700,000. Even if we consider only the permanently bedfast, there appear to be far more of them living in private households than in all institutions combined.

TABLE 4

Personal incapacity of persons aged 65 and over living at home and in institutions; Britain 1962-1963

(samples of 4,183 in private households and of 2,205 in institutions)

| Personal incapacity (score) | Private households | | | | | |
| | Men | | Women | | Men and women | |
	%	Estimated number	%	Estimated number	%	Estimated number
None or slight (0–2)	83·5	1,980,600	71·2	2,526,200	76·1	4,505,100
Moderate (3–6) ...	10·9	258,600	17·4	617,300	14·8	876,200
Severe (7+) ...	4·2	99,600	8·9	315,800	7·0	414,400
Bedfast	1·4	33,200	2·5	88,700	2·1	124,300
Total	100·0	2,372,000	100·0	3,548,000	100·0	5,920,000
	Institutions					
None or slight (0–2)	38·4	32,200	22·1	43,300	27·1	75,900
Moderate (3–6) ...	21·9	18,400	19·7	38,600	20·3	56,800
Severe (7+) ...	20·9	17,600	29·2	57,200	26·7	74,800
Bedfast	18·8	15,800	29·0	56,900	25·9	72,500
Total	100·0	84,000	100·0	196,000	100·0	280,000

Note: A total of 4,067 in private households were interviewed, but information was given about a further 116 old people by proxies. Among these two groups 51 and 3 respectively were unclassifiable so far as incapacity was concerned. Among the 2,205 in institutions 11 were unclassifiable. Estimates of population numbers are subject to sampling error (Appendix 2).

Much the same kind of paradox arises from the data on home help and meals services. Although a significantly higher proportion

---

1. A second measure of household incapacity was also developed, which depended on four questions —whether the old person could do *light housework*, like washing up and dusting, *heavy housework*, like washing floors and cleaning windows, *make a cup of tea or coffee* and *prepare a hot meal*. The results of applying both measures independently and together will be described in the forthcoming full report.

of the people receiving than not receiving each home service were severely or moderately incapacitated, there were some recipients in the sample who were only slightly incapacitated. Moreover, there were substantial numbers of severely incapacitated people, some of whom were living alone, who did not receive any of the public services. To explain this we need to explore their social status and condition.

The family status of persons in institutions and at home

Do many old persons in institutions have families who could care for them? A full answer to this question would have to draw on detailed information about relatives, based possibly on direct interviews with them, and our information was chiefly confined to the existence and nearness of immediate members of the family. Thirty-three per cent of all old persons in our institutional sample were unmarried; 26 per cent of those who were married or widowed were childless, and 39 per cent of those who had children had one only. These figures compare with 10 per cent, 16 per cent and 26 per cent respectively of persons in the private households sample, as Table 5 shows.

In addition we found that 30 per cent of the institutional sample, compared with 22 per cent of the private household sample, had no surviving brothers and sisters. This series of comparisons means not only that the institutional population contains a disproportionately large number of unmarried and, to a lesser extent, of widowed persons—a fact which is already well known. It means that the institutional population differs markedly from the population living at home in all major aspects of family structure. Perhaps the most important general point is that a total of 49 per cent of those in institutions (54 per cent in psychiatric hospitals), compared with 24 per cent at home, were childless (including the unmarried).

It would seem that there is a marked inverse correlation between the number of close relatives that a person has (spouse, children, brothers and sisters) and the likelihood that he will enter an institution in his old age. When incapacity is also taken into account this correlation becomes more marked, but two further variables seem to be important—the sex of close relatives and *their* incapacity. A disproportionately large number of those with children in the institutional sample had sons only and though we collected no statistical information about the incapacity of close relatives, we noted that in interviews and in case-records infirm relatives were often mentioned. Case-records referred to infirm husbands or wives, and sometimes an only child was referred to as being in a hospital, or lying ill at home.

There are nonetheless a substantial number in the institutional population who do have children or brothers and sisters. Our evidence is that they are people who have not been in such close touch during their lives with their relatives as most old people. We obtained information about the nearness of relatives before the admission of those persons who were in institutions. More had lived further than ten minutes journey from the nearest child or sibling. So the family

TABLE 5

Marital and family status of persons aged 65 and over living in institutions and at home; Britain 1962-1963

| Marital or family status | Old persons living in | | | | | |
| | Institutions | | | Private households | | |
	Men	Women	Men and women	Men	Women	Men and women
1. Unmarried ...	% 32	% 34	% 33	% 4	% 14	% 10
Married or widowed ...	68	66	67	96	86	90
Total (1)	100	100	100	100	100	100
2. Married or widowed but childless (2)	24	28	26	16	16	16
Married or widowed with children (3)	76	72	74	84	84	84
Total	100	100	100	100	100	100
3. Married or widowed with children, 1 only ...	40	38	39	28	25	26
Married or widowed with children, more than 1	60	62	61	72	75	74
Total	100	100	100	100	100	100
Numbers in sample	672	1,523	2,195	1,629	2,436	4,065

Note:
(1) Unclassifiable, 10 in the institution sample of 2,205; 2 in the private household sample of 4,067 ('proxy' informants excluded).
(2) Married or widowed also includes divorced and formally or informally separated.
(3) Unmarried women with children are not of course included. (They numbered 5 and 9 respectively in the two samples.)

is not only less complete or well knit in structure; it is also more fragmented geographically.

Finally, among the institutional population significantly less of those without children were severely incapacitated (including the bedfast), as shown in Table 6. This suggests that old people with children reach a more advanced stage of infirmity than others before seeking (or being granted) admission to different kinds of institution. The reader should, of course, remember that people who have lived for many years in the institutions are included in the table. If newly admitted residents and patients alone were considered the differences in incapacity between the childless and those with children might be more striking.

TABLE 6
Incapacity of persons aged 65 and over in institutions who possess or do not possess surviving children; Britain 1963

(institution sub-sample of 1,102)

Personal incapacity (score)	Persons aged 65 and over		
	No children	One child only	More than one child
	%	%	%
None or slight (0–2)	28·4	25·1	21·0
Moderate (3–6)	24·2	13·4	22·2
Severe (7+)	27·3	32·6	27·1
Bedfast	20·2	28·9	29·7
Total	100·0	100·0	100·0
Number	550	187	347

Note: Unclassifiable, 18.

The family status of persons receiving and not receiving domiciliary social services

When we turn to consider the family characteristics of people who are or who are not receiving public and voluntary home services, similar conclusions can be drawn, though the data allow us to consider other social characteristics as well. In the sample there were, excluding the bedfast,[1] 172 persons, or 4·2 per cent, who were visited by a local authority home help. A third of them (33 per cent) were severely and a half (52 per cent) moderately incapacitated.[2] Nearly half (49 per cent) lived alone and nearly half, again, did not have any relatives living with them or within ten minutes journey of their homes. Indeed two-fifths of the recipients (42 per cent) were both incapacitated *and* living entirely alone. There were only five of the 172 persons who stated that they had no difficulty in doing heavy housework. The others stated that they had difficulty, or could not do it at all. Table 7 gives examples of the differences between the recipients of welfare services and others.

More women than men in the sample were visited by local authority home helps (4·6 per cent compared with 3·6 per cent) and of these two minorities more of the women were infirm, lived alone and were isolated from their relatives. At an early stage of infirmity unmarried and widowed men are more likely to seek, and be given, help than unmarried and widowed women. However, many fewer men than women in the population are unmarried or widowed or infirm and this fact reduces what would otherwise be a marked difference between the sexes in the use made of the services.

1. The information obtained from bedfast people had to be restricted and although 9 of them were assisted by a home help and are counted in the overall total given in Table 2, they have had to be excluded from the subsequent analysis described here.
2. In the strict sense defined earlier, but taking account of capacity to undertake four household tasks (making a cup of tea or coffee, preparing a meal and doing light and heavy housework) as well as capacity to undertake six personal tasks (walk outdoors, walk indoors, negotiate stairs, wash and bath, dress, and cut toe-nails).

TABLE 7

Percentage of persons receiving and not receiving public or private domestic help who had certain characteristics; Britain, 1962

Characteristics	Local authority home help	Privately paid domestic help	Neither local authority nor privately paid help
Total number (1)	172	367	3,467
	%	%	%
Moderately or severely incapacitated (2)	85	33	30
Living alone	49	27	21
Childless	34	39	22
Children, but none living at home or nearby (ten minutes journey) (3)...	52	39	35
No relatives living at home or nearby	49	39	31
Social Classes I and II (4) ...	9	56	14
Social Class V	12	2	13
Reporting difficulty with heavy housework	97	66	44

Note:
(1) 61 unclassifiable.
(2) 125 unclassifiable for incapacity.
(3) Percentages only of those with children.
(4) 270 unclassifiable. Social Class as defined by the Registrar-General.

Only 46 persons, or 1 per cent of the sample, had a cooked meal delivered at least once a week by the mobile meals service. It is difficult to say very much about this small number. But it is of some interest that half of the 20 men and three-quarters of the 26 women lived alone. Nearly all the women as well as over half the men were moderately or severely incapacitated. More than a third of them had no children (including 8 who had no relatives at all) and of those who did have children, more than half had neither a child nor any other relative living within ten minutes journey of their homes.

Characteristics of all recipients of the domiciliary services

Much the same could be said of some other services. When we took account of all those in the sample who were receiving help with personal or household affairs from one or more of the public or voluntary home services—home help, meals, district nursing, chiropody, laundry, bathing—we found that 11·8 per cent were involved, representing nearly 700,000 persons in the elderly population. More of the women than of the men, 13·9 per cent compared with 8·8 per cent, were receiving one or more services.[1] It is possible that

1. The figures do not take account of the small numbers of the bedfast in the sample. If adjusted to include them, they would be 12·1 per cent, 14·8 per cent and 9·0 per cent respectively. They have been excluded to avoid confusion. Although they can be incorporated in our totals, they cannot be incorporated into different sub-categories.

some beneficiaries of certain services, such as health visiting and day centres, are not included in our total. Our questions were not comprehensive. On the other hand, in asking a range of questions about help with personal and household affairs it was possible for individuals to reply by naming particular services, even though questions were asked specifically only about nursing, home help, meals and chiropody services. The figure of 11·8 per cent is unlikely to be far short of the true proportion of old people benefiting from one or more of the home services in 1962.

How can their characteristics be summarised? As one would expect, far more of the persons in their eighties than of the persons in their sixties were recipients of the social services. Table 8 shows how the proportion increased steadily with age, reaching 23 per cent of those aged 85 and over.

TABLE 8

Percentage of old people of different age receiving at least one domiciliary social service; Britain 1962

Age					Men	Women	Men and women
65–66	...	...	...	...	1·9	8·9	4·7
67–69	...	...	...	...	5·3	9·1	7·8
70–74	...	...	...	...	7·6	12·9	10·5
75–79	...	...	...	...	14·6	17·6	16·4
80–84	...	...	...	...	22·1	21·4	21·7
85+	...	...	...	...	15·0	26·5	22·8
All ages 65+	...	...	...	...	8·8	13·3	11·8

Second, more of them were incapacitated, 20 per cent being severely incapacitated and a further 48 per cent moderately incapacitated, compared with 7 per cent and 22 per cent respectively of those not receiving help.

Third, as one might also expect, more of them were poor. Analysis of income and social class reveals a number of interesting features. More of those receiving services than of the non-recipients were unmarried or widowed women and, as a group, these tended to be poorer than unmarried or widowed men and poorer also than married couples. In addition, whether they were single or married, significantly more of them fell into the lowest income groups. Thirty-five per cent of the single recipients had a total income of less than £3 10s. a week (and 86 per cent less than £5 10s. a week). Thirty-four per cent of the married couple recipients had less than £6 per week (and 81 per cent less than £9 per week). There is one interesting exception, however. It would seem that slightly fewer of the poorest widowed and single women (with incomes below £3 10s. a week) were receiving domiciliary services. The chief explanation is that those who lived alone tended to receive both domiciliary services *and* supplementary national assistance (which, with their pensions took their incomes above £3 10s. a week). Many of those with less than £3 10s. a week were living with relatives, and, simply because they were living with them, were less likely also to be getting domiciliary services.

But two matters should be noted. Some of those with higher incomes were getting services.[1] Also, old people belonging to the Registrar-General's Social Classes IV and V depended little more than average on the social services. Table 9 shows that the largest proportion of those using domiciliary services were old people whose former occupations (or, if women, whose husbands' former occupations) had been skilled manual. The proportions using the public social services were much more evenly distributed among the different social classes (with the exception of professional groups in Social Class I) than is commonly supposed. It would be interesting to find whether individuals in the different social classes enjoyed, on average, the same *extent* of service (in terms of numbers of visits, or expenditure of time or money).

TABLE 9

Percentage of old people of different social class who were receiving at least one domiciliary social service; Britain 1962

Social Class	Per cent receiving at least one domiciliary service	Total numbers in sample
I Professional	3·7	82
II Managerial	9·0	557
IIIaSkilled non-manual	9·7	401
IIIbSkilled manual	15·4	1,199
IV Semi-skilled	12·9	1,044
V Unskilled	12·6	453
All Classes	11·8	3,736

Note: Formerly armed services or no occupation 53 (5 receiving at least one service), unclassifiable (nearly all women), 278 (20 receiving at least one service).

Fourth, more of the old people receiving the home services were socially isolated either because they lacked children and other relatives or because they were separated from them. Thirty-nine per cent lived alone, compared with 20 per cent of those not receiving services. Thirty per cent were childless, compared with 22 per cent. Forty-one per cent did not have any relatives living within 10 minutes journey compared with 31 per cent. Table 10 also shows the importance of family proximity. Significantly fewer of those with children living at home or nearby were receiving social services than of those who had no relatives or none within ten minutes journey.

1. In some parts of the country a charge is made for home-help services, depending on a means test So at least some of those with higher incomes paid a contribution for the services they received

TABLE 10

Percentage of old persons with relatives at home, nearby, or at a distance who were receiving at least one domiciliary social service; Britain 1962

Proximity of Relatives	per cent receiving at least one domiciliary service	Total numbers in sample
Children living at home	7·7	1,292
Other relatives living at home ...	9·6	396
No relatives at home, children living near	13·3	633
No relatives at home, other relatives living near	14·2	445
No relatives at home or living near ...	15·2	1,300
All distances	11·8	4,066

Note: Unclassifiable, 1. 'Living near' defined as within 10 minutes journey of the home.

Summary

We began this chapter by showing that while there is wide agreement about the desirability of helping old people to stay in their own homes, little evidence has emerged of more emphasis being given to the home as compared with the institutional services. We went on to describe the numbers and kinds of people using the different services. Our data showed that in 1962–63 about 4½ per cent of persons aged 65 and over lived in institutions and about 12 per cent received domiciliary health and welfare services (excluding medical care). As one would expect, more of those in institutions than of those living at home were bedfast or otherwise severely incapacitated (though it seems that more than half a million such people are living at home). But they differed strikingly in other ways from the population living at home. Far more were unmarried, more lacked children and brothers and sisters, and more of those who had children had only one or had sons rather than daughters. More of those in the institutional population who had close relatives were separated from them and had led isolated lives. To a lesser extent such findings applied also to those receiving social services at home as compared with the rest of the elderly population living at home. More of them were incapacitated, lived alone and lacked available relatives. Although more of them also had very low incomes, as one would expect, this correlation was not so marked as is often assumed. The proportions of different social classes using the services were not dissimilar, with the exception of the professional classes, who depended much more heavily on privately paid domestic and professional help.

There is not much evidence so far of health and welfare services being 'misused' or 'undermining' family responsibilities. Rather, it appears that many of those who benefit from services are persons who lack a family or have none within reach.

32

CHAPTER 2

The Role of the Family in Illness and Infirmity

To show that the institutional and domiciliary health and welfare services tend to reach those who in old age lack close relatives or have none available is only a first, though an important, step in the analysis of the practical and theoretical relationship of the family and the Welfare State. How big is the family's role? It is possible to imagine a universal disruption of the relationship between, say, the elderly and their adult children, so that the ordinary functions of furnishing care in illness and infirmity are not carried out. How much larger would the social services have to be? Alternatively, it is possible to imagine persons other than members of the family carrying out services traditionally performed by the family. Publicly employed bathing attendants and laundry workers might visit the home each week. Or welfare assistants might take old people in special cars to 'Darby and Joan' salons to be fitted out with stylish and comfortable clothes, or to have their feet and hands attended to, or to be shaved or have their hair dressed. Many things for old people *might* be done better, or more efficiently, than they are today by the family. Is this in fact true, and of what?

The national survey was not designed to provide answers to the whole series of questions which might be prompted by this line of thought, but it gives a framework of knowledge about the *extent* of family activity and the points at which the demand or need for different professional services is beginning to complicate the division of labour within the households and families of which old people are members. Community services must no longer be thought of simply as *replacing* the services of the family or *substituting* for them when they cannot exist—though this is one primary role. They must also be increasingly thought of as *supplementing* or *complementing* those services. This is the theme of this chapter. We shall briefly discuss the general role of the family in relation to professional social services and then go on to describe the *extent* of family help given to the aged in illness and infirmity.

The family and the social services

Sociological theorists of the changes that have taken place in the family during industrialisation in the nineteenth and twentieth centuries frequently assume that certain functions formerly performed by the family have been taken over by other social institutions—particularly by the social services of local and central government.

Changes in the activities of different individuals in the family before and after the introduction of public services have not been analysed, however, and in fact the relationship between the family and the Welfare State is much more subtle than has been implied. We can understand this if we consider, for example, the provision of nursing and chiropody care for old people.

In the nineteenth century, developments in scientific medicine, and particularly the knowledge that was accumulating of the dangers of infection, helped to prompt the creation of a professional cadre of nurses. There were circumstances when a specially trained person had greater success with sick patients than untrained relatives or women of the village. This is equally true today with the care of elderly patients. Injections may have to be given, a strict medical régime followed, or special techniques to cure bedsores used. Special knowledge may also be needed to help relatives avoid becoming fearful, distressed or unsympathetic about the course and form of illness. These are some of the justifications for having trained nurses working in the community. But we should not necessarily assume that they are *replacing* the family in nursing the elderly. First, they may be carrying out tasks which the family would never, from ignorance or lack of skill, have previously performed. Second, they may be unable, from shortage of recruits, to supply the constant attention which many elderly patients require and may be unable to do much more than guide the family and boost its morale. It was evident from individual instances in our sample, particularly among the bedfast, that the role of the district nurse was primarily one of complementing the role of the family rather than of *replacing* it, though sometimes, of course, for elderly patients who had no relatives or scarcely any, she *substituted* for it.

The development of chiropody treatment for the elderly is an interesting modern example of the professionalisation of certain services because of new knowledge. It is gradually becoming appreciated not only that a large number of the elderly have particular difficulty in caring for their feet, but also that foot troubles can reduce mobility and have many kinds of unfortunate psychological and social consequences. It is felt that persons trained to recognise and treat disorders of the feet should also examine those of old people regularly. But this opinion is taking time to spread. Chiropody has not yet been established as a key preventive measure within the practice of modern geriatrics and some old people and their relatives do not yet recognise that it should be done professionally rather than by themselves. But at the same time, however, it should be remembered that developments in public education and in the communication of values and techniques through the mass media may also be raising the standards of care provided for old people by relatives, compared with the standards practised by previous generations. In other words, the family may be doing some of its work better than it used to. This probably also means that it may be doing more of certain kinds of work than it used to.

Besides furnishing expert professional help which the family cannot supply, there is another sense in which the Welfare State *complements* the role of the family in caring for the aged. It may fill some or all of the gaps in the unskilled or semi-skilled services that are already available. Thus, even when relatives are living at home, it may be justified to provide some welfare services. For example, a son or husband may be at work in the day and be unable to get meals.

Mrs Canley[1], aged 73, has been separated from her husband for many years and she lives in the West Riding with her only child, a bachelor son of 53, who goes to work on weekdays from 8 until 5. She is bedfast. "I feel very useless now. I can't do anything for myself. I had a stroke and my back is paralysed. I've had a few heart attacks since then, so I'm no good for anything. I can't do anything at all but just lie here. They are long days and I don't like being dependent on other people". A council home help calls each day and meals are delivered by the WVS on two days of the week. A district nurse also calls each day and her general practitioner about once a month. Her son pays all household expenses. She used to work in a textile factory and later in a school canteen. "I think people visiting would be nice. Its lonely when you are bedfast. They should come and see how you're getting on".

Among our sample there were, of course, many other instances of relatives living at home who were not themselves able to do all that might be needed. There were husbands or wives who were infirm, a sister who was mentally subnormal, a daughter who was a spastic and even a number of daughters and sons who were themselves of pensionable age. Much the same was true of relatives living near old people who lived alone. There were many who saw old people frequently and gave some and even considerable help and yet needed supporting help from the social services.

Mrs Pennyhall is a widow of 75 living alone in a Victorian house in an East Anglian town. She rarely goes out of doors and hadn't done so for three months during the winter. She had a severe stroke two years ago and went to live with her married daughter, who lives eight minutes walk away, for three months. One of her hands was badly affected by the stroke and now she finds it difficult to wash and dress. Her daughter calls on her twice every day, first to do the shopping and get the coal up before going to work in a local factory, and then between shifts. A district nurse comes once a week and among other things washes Mrs Pennyhall's feet and cuts her toenails. The WVS mobile meals service delivers meals (which cost tenpence) on Tuesdays

---

1. In giving illustrations in this report, names and one or two other particulars have been changed to conceal individual identity.

and Thursdays. (Fortunately, she is visited first in the round and the meals are hot.) She would like to have them more often. Her daughter and a neighbour do the heavy cleaning between them. She receives £1 2s. supplementary national assistance per week and during the winter an additional 5s. per week for extra fuel. "My roots are here. If you took me away, I'd be lost".

These examples suggest some of the ways in which the Welfare State already supports the family and thereby enables an old person who might otherwise have to enter a residential institution or hospital to go on living at home.

The role of the family in illness

How far do old people depend for certain services on the family rather than on the Welfare State? Care given in illness is clearly important and nearly a third of the sample had been ill at home during the previous twelve months. Table 11 shows the main sources of help with housework, shopping and meals at that time.[1] Husbands and wives and children proved to be the predominant sources of help, as one might expect. Altogether 77 per cent of those who had been ill at home relied on a spouse, children or other relatives for help with housework, 80 per cent with shopping and 82 per cent for help with

TABLE 11

Percentage of persons ill in bed last year who received different kinds of help from different sources; Britain 1962

Source of help	Persons ill in bed last year		
	Receiving help with housework	Receiving help with shopping	Receiving help with meals
	%	%	%
Spouse	30·5	30·3	35·6
Child in household	22·2	22·2	21·6
Child outside household	13·2	15·1	12·9
Relative in household	6·7	7·2	7·1
Relative outside household ...	4·1	4·9	3·9
Other in household	2·2	2·1	2·2
Friend or neighbour	3·2	9·7	5·9
Social services	4·8	1·8	1·4
Private domestic help	4·8	1·7	1·6
Other help outside	0·9	1·4	0·9
None	7·3	3·5	7·0
Total	100·0	100·0	100·0
Number	1,159	1,160	1,161

Note: Nearly 3,000 persons not ill in bed in previous year excluded. Information not available for 18, 17 and 16 persons respectively.

1. Shopping and housework are sometimes done by more than one person and we attempted to obtain information only about the main source of help.

meals. But two other conclusions can be drawn from the table. One is that substantial proportions of old people (up to a third) rely in time of illness on help from children and other relatives, and some of them upon friends, who live elsewhere than in the household. Second, the role of the social services in personal and household care is small. In illness they serve a minority of roughly the same size as that depending on privately paid domestic help.

Family help with personal and household affairs

We have described the help available to old people in time of illness in bed. From whom do they obtain help ordinarily with personal and household affairs? A multitude of different activities might be investigated and we confined ourselves to those which frequently gave difficulty to the elderly. Persons saying they were unable to bath themselves (or give themselves a wash-down at a sink), for example, made up 6 per cent of the sample. Table 12 shows that a half depended on a spouse, a child or another relative living at home. But it is of particular interest that nearly 1 in 10 were helped by a child, another relative or a friend living elsewhere than in the household. A minority of 7 per cent depended on the social services.

TABLE 12

Percentage of persons being unable to bath themselves even with difficulty, who received help in bathing from different sources; Britain 1962

Source of help in bathing	Persons being unable to bath		
	Men	Women	Men and women
	%	%	%
Spouse	44	11	19
Child in household	25	25	25
Child outside household	3	4	4
Relative in household	5	7	6
Relative outside household	2	3	3
Others in household	—	—	—
Friend or neighbour	—	2	2
Social services	5	7	7
Private domestic help	—	—	—
Others outside household	—	—	—
None	19	55	46
Total	104	114	112
Number of persons	57	185	242
Number of replies	59	205	264

Note: Seven women, who were unable to bath themselves, gave no information on source of help.

Nearly a half of those who said they were unable to bath themselves also said that no one helped them to bath. Our interviews unfortunately included no further questions which would have allowed us to find how they overcame their difficulties. Some old people strive to the point of obstinacy to preserve their independence, and they will even pretend to their closest relatives and friends that they are able to do things for themselves which in fact are now beyond their capacities. This is particularly true of personal toilet, and relatives will even join them in a kind of conspiracy to preserve the myth of their independence. Some are in a transitional stage between states of independence and dependence and would rather have nothing done for them, for some time at least—with all the disastrous consequences this implies in terms of deterioration in standards of personal and household cleanliness. So either they try to conceal from their own families the fact that their struggles with a soapy flannel don't really amount to a wash-down or they grudgingly accept help without anyone being ready to call it help. Occasionally, so far as bathing is concerned, an old person is ready to be helped but cannot accept it from the particular relatives who are available (especially if they are of the opposite sex) or would only accept professional help from outside, with the family kept out of the picture.

With one exception, Table 12 provides a representative example of the pattern of help received by old people for other activities involving personal toilet and care. The exception is care of the feet. This tends to be taken for granted by the young, but in later life foot disorders can easily develop and lead to immobility unless corns, hard skin and toenails can be regularly attended to. We could not ask detailed questions and confined ourselves to the difficulties old people

TABLE 13

Percentage of persons being unable to care for their feet even with difficulty who received help with such care from different sources; Britain 1962

Source of help	Persons being unable to cut toenails		
	Men	Women	Men and women
	%	%	%
Spouse	33	8	15
Child in household	17	13	14
Child outside household	4	7	7
Relative in household	2	3	3
Relative outside household	0	3	2
Others in household	2	1	1
Friends and neighbours	2	2	2
Social service	23	29	27
Private domestic help	—	—	—
Others outside household (including private chiropodist)	11	28	23
None	5	6	6
Total	101	101	101
Number of persons	185	504	689
Number of replies	186	509	695

Note: One woman, who was unable to care for her feet, gave no information on source of help.

had in cutting toenails—which previous research had shown to be common. Altogether, as many as 17 per cent of the elderly said they were unable to cut their own toenails. Table 13 shows that of these a quarter were helped by the social services and another quarter by 'others outside the household' (nearly all of them private chiropodists).

We also asked the old people about help with household management—preparing meals, making a cup of tea or coffee, and doing light and heavy housework. Of those saying they had difficulty in doing heavy housework (who numbered nearly half of the entire sample), 61 per cent depended on husbands or wives, children and other relatives for help. A fact worthy of note is that nearly a fifth depended on relatives or friends living outside the home.

> Mrs Furneach is a widow of 86 living alone in a terraced house, with a W.C. in the yard, in an eastern suburb of London. She has kidney trouble and a district nurse calls on her each week. Her general practitioner visits about once a month and in the previous twelve months she had a total of 63 nights in hospital. One of her five married daughters lives opposite and two others live less than an hour's journey away. "My eldest girl (who is aged 65) does everything for me. She cooks for me, looks after my pension and shops and washes for me".

> Miss Thirlton is aged 75 and lives alone in a Nottinghamshire town. She has lived at the same address for 60 years and used to be a machinist hemming scarves. She walks with great difficulty with a stick and, according to our definition, is on the borderline of moderate and severe incapacity. Although she has difficulty in dressing, she said she did not need help. She would have moved to a modern bungalow years before but for her sister, who lives a few houses along in the same road and "pops in two or three times a day" to help her with housework and shopping. Her legs are painful because of varicose veins, and her sister accompanies her regularly to the outpatients' department of a local hospital for treatment. A niece who also lives nearby visits frequently.

There were another 8 per cent who depended on the social services and 11 per cent on privately paid domestic help. But as many as 13 per cent had no help. Even of those who could not do heavy housework at all, 5 per cent said they had no help. Table 14 shows the proportions dependent on different sources of help.

For the smaller proportion of old people who had difficulty in preparing a meal (1 in 10) the pattern of help was even more strongly woven by the family. Relatively fewer were dependent on private domestic help and fewer upon the social services. Only 2 per cent of the men and 6 per cent of the women saying they had difficulty in preparing meals in fact were helped by the social services. They accounted for sixteen people in the entire sample of 4,067, or less than ½ per cent.

TABLE 14

Percentage of persons having difficulty in doing heavy housework, who received help with housework from different sources; Britain 1962

Source of help	Persons having difficulty with heavy housework		
	Men	Women	Men and women
	%	%	%
Spouse	37	11	19
Child in household	20	26	24
Child outside household	8	12	10
Relative in household	4	6	5
Relative outside household	2	3	3
Others in household	3	2	2
Friends and neighbours	1	3	3
Social service	8	9	8
Private domestic help	10	12	11
Others outside	3	7	6
None	7	16	13
Total	103	107	104
Number of persons	625	1,296	1,921
Number of replies	651	1,366	2,017

Note: Unclassifiable, 19 persons.

TABLE 15

Percentage of persons having difficulty in preparing hot meals, who received help with their meals from different sources; Britain 1962

Source of help	Persons having difficulty in preparing meals		
	Men	Women	Men and women
	%	%	%
Spouse	59	15	39
Child in household	22	38	29
Child outside household	2	6	4
Relative in household	5	13	9
Relative outside household	1	2	1
Others in household	2	2	2
Friends and neighbours	3	5	4
Social services	2	6	4
Private domestic help	0	4	2
Others outside	0	0	0
None	5	15	10
Total	101	106	104
Number of persons	235	188	423
Number of replies	243	200	443

Note: Unclassifiable, 17 persons.

Family help for the bedfast at home

In discussing the care provided for old people living at home we have so far left out a small but extremely important minority of about 2 per cent who are permanently bedfast. As shown in the previous chapter this minority is larger in absolute numbers than the bedfast in hospitals and other institutions and deserves very close study. Certainly a special survey of such persons would seem to be justified. Our information about these individuals in our sample is not as full as it is for others, and was often supplied by a proxy—which explains why it is discussed separately.

Altogether there were 79 persons in the sample who were bedfast at home. Some of these had entered their terminal illness or were acutely ill or disabled and otherwise needed continuous nursing. One man of 70 who suffered from disseminated sclerosis could not move any of his limbs and was lifted and washed and fed by his wife. Although the general practitioner called twice a week, he was not visited by personnel from any of the domiciliary social services. There were other elderly wives who undertook a severe burden of nursing, but often they gained support from relatives and friends, who did the shopping and cleaning if not personal nursing. One man of 76 in an extreme condition of emaciation was cared for by his 80 years old wife, but a daughter did the cleaning and a neighbour some of the shopping.

Often a widow or widower was cared for by the children.

Mrs Pryden is a widow of 76 living in a Midlands town with a married daughter and son-in-law in their forties. Until a year previously she kept house elsewhere for her two sons, but she became ill with lung cancer, had a short spell in hospital and stayed with another married daughter, who nursed her, for six months. She is now extremely emaciated and breathes heavily and was moved to join this daughter for the last months of her life. A district nurse and her general practitioner each pay a routine visit once a week but otherwise she receives no social services. She has three sons and four daughters and sees one of the latter, in addition to the daughter at home, every day. Three of the other children visit at least every week and the other two at least once a month. She murmured that she wanted to stay in this home but generally she thought that "there should be more homes for the old where they could have their own rooms and be looked after by experienced staff, and also hospitals for the old and bedridden who live on their own". One interesting fact is that she said her health was fair for her age.

Sometimes other relatives provided care.

Mrs Hoyell is a widow of 80 years who has no children and who lives with a niece of 43 and her three children in a Lancashire town near Manchester. She is bedfast and is very frail and thin.

41

She has had one or two strokes and speaking is a great effort, because she also suffers from bronchitis. But apart from being visited occasionally by her general practitioner, she is not visited by any of the social services. Her niece 'does everything'— shopping, cooking, washing, bathing and so on. A great-niece visits occasionally to attend to her feet. To the interviewer the niece seemed 'gentle and devoted'.

Mr Cutright is 90 years old and he lives with his widowed daughter-in-law of 63. She cooks for him and looks after him in every way in an old Victorian house which has an outside W.C. A district nurse visits once a week. Mr Cutright has been bedfast for two or three years and, to give some relief to his daughter-in-law, he goes into a local hospital for three or four weeks every year and is taken to spend some weekends with two children living elsewhere.

Only a third of the 79 bedfast persons received skilled nursing help regularly (mostly through the council district nursing service). Nearly all of these were visited at least once a week, many of them twice or several times a week, by a nurse. Over half the bedfast were visited regularly by the doctor (usually every month or fortnight but sometimes once a week or more) and another quarter of them 'occasionally'. Ten, or 1 in 8, had a council home help and a few were visited by a chiropodist. But the great majority relied on their families for personal and household care and even for basic nursing. A spouse, a child, or another relative living in the household was the main source of help with housework, meals and shopping for nearly four-fifths, and a child or another relative living elsewhere for another 1 in 10. For these everyday tasks fewer than 1 in 20 depended on privately paid domestic help and fewer than 1 in 10 on the social services.

Summary

It seems that the domiciliary services perform two main positive functions. They furnish expert professional help which the family cannot supply, and they furnish unskilled or semi-skilled help for persons who do not have families or whose families living in the household or nearby are not always able or available to help. But the extent to which they fulfil this second function, in relation to the total task of caring for the aged, should be kept in proportion. We have presented evidence in this chapter showing that in some things, such as the preparation of meals during illness at home (Table 11), the family helps nearly 60 times as many persons as the social services. In providing regular care of the feet, on the other hand, which is rapidly becoming the responsibility of qualified chiropodists, the margin is reduced to less than twice as many persons. Nonetheless, the evidence shows that in illness and infirmity the role of the family in providing personal and household care dwarfs that of the social services. While in very general terms this may seem to be a very straightforward conclusion, it does, of course, have serious social implications. The development of public housing policies which make it difficult for relatives of different generations to obtain housing near to one another or of transport policies which make it difficult for them to communicate are likely to result in much greater pressures on the social services. There are considerable social costs in overlooking the existence and the functions of the extended family in modern society.

But, equally, the limitations of intra-family relationships must not be ignored. Persons who live together can sometimes have a stultifying effect on each other's talents or can unwittingly do each other harm. In personal or household crises much may depend on expert knowledge and skill, as well as forbearance. Uneducated expressions of love and loyalty are crucially important in many of life's situations, but not all. We have too little information on the quality of care provided for old people by their families at home. One problem is to equip the family to do this task better (through specially designed housing and constant attendance allowances in sickness, for example). Another is to raise the general level of education and thereby general standards of personal and household care.

CHAPTER 3

Evidence for Expansion of Services

Having shown that some of the principal health and welfare services for the aged tend to serve the more isolated sections of the population and also in other ways complement, rather than compete with or replace, the family, we reach the third step of our analysis. Is there considerable scope nonetheless for expansion of the services? There are a number of related but distinct questions. Is there any evidence (i) that more people need to receive certain services; (ii) that present recipients need more of the same services, and (iii) that people have a need for services which have yet to be introduced? Data on the second and third of these questions were not specifically sought during the national survey though general information about infirmity and availability of relatives and friends was, of course, obtained. This should be borne in mind in the subsequent analysis.

The concept of need

How is it possible to find whether more people 'need' a particular service? The concept of need is not easy to explore. We can ask old people if they would like to have a service, or whether they feel they need it, which is not quite the same thing. But should we accept what they say or make an independent assessment of their situation as well? Some people who plead for support may be quite capable of continuing to manage for themselves. Others who protest their independence may be in serious need of help. Indeed, it is sometimes difficult to decide what in fact their attitude is. People who are becoming infirm are often uncertain of the extent of their capacities and this uncertainty may be reflected in different opinions given on succeeding days, or even within the compass of a single interview. Another problem is that many people only have the haziest idea of what in fact a particular service consists of and, without giving some information, it is hard to expect them to come to a considered judgment. But this is a common problem—perhaps the basic problem in all social studies which attempt to gauge attitudes. Without ascertaining the varying width of social experience of people being asked standard attitude questions, and even without making sure that the standard questions mean roughly the same thing to most of the people being questioned, the answers are of doubtful value. Information is not acquired evenly by all sections of the population. Nor are social norms and expectations uniformly interpreted. Certainly the expectations of the older generation seem to lag behind those of younger generations.

Independent assessment of their situation also involves a number of problems. Rules for the external determination of need have to be drawn very wide even to begin to cover individual situations. Some people live alone; others do not. Some live in squalid backstreet tenements, others in cottages with a W.C. at the end of the garden, and others in large town houses. Some are near shopping and other facilities; others are remote from them. Some are frail but capable of doing most things for themselves; others have particular disabilities which limit specific activities. People differ in these and many other ways and if rational decisions about whether they need help are to be made, then questions have to be asked not only about infirmity and the availability of help, but also income, housing, the nearness of particular kinds of shops, the frequency of a bus service, and so on. This can quickly become a complicated exercise. In a variety of ways the individual's condition and his circumstances have to be compared with the conditions and circumstances of other individuals in the same society (a) of like age and sex and (b) of a different generation. They also have to be compared with (c) the conditions and circumstances which were experienced by the individual at an earlier age. In sociological terms 'need' can only be revealed systematically by calling up the concepts of 'reference group' and 'referred experience'.

Even when an exercise of this kind is completed the answer to the practical question 'does this individual need help?' may depend on a number of hidden assumptions: that the service has to be restricted on grounds of cost or limited manpower to a particular number of people, that the family should normally be expected or obliged to provide care, that with few exceptions individuals should be obliged even in old age, to be self-reliant in at least some respects. These are not just individual value assumptions. More often they are the value assumptions of society or at least of certain sections of the population, though the individual welfare worker or administrator may stress some rather than others. There is a big difference, in short, between assessing individual needs according to rational criteria and laying down standards of provision of services. All this should help us to be cautious in generalising about need.

The local authority home help service

Compared with the minority of 4·4 per cent (4·2 per cent excluding the bedfast) who were served by local authority home helps at the time of the survey, another 5·7 per cent did not have privately paid help and said they needed "someone to come in and help with the housework". The proportion feeling the need for help was the same for each sex. They represented about 332,000 old people in the population.

Of the minority feeling a need for help (numbering 230 in the sample) 73 per cent said they had difficulty in doing heavy housework or could not do it at all, and a third of these people claimed they had no-one to help them at the present time. Fifty-seven per cent were moderately or severely incapacitated, 35 per cent were childless and 30 per cent were living entirely alone. As many as 35 per cent had no relatives living with them or within ten minutes journey. Each of these figures is significantly larger than the comparable figure for those in the sample not seeking help.

One interesting feature of our results which deserves further inquiry is the difference in attitude between incapacitated people of different social class. Nearly half those in Social Classes I and II[1] who were severely incapacitated already had privately paid or local authority domestic help, and nearly half the others said they needed help. But only a sixth of those in Social Class V who were severely incapacitated had such help already and only a fifth of the remainder felt the need for it. Table 16 shows the distribution according to source of help for all persons in the sample, whether incapacitated or not. There is a very steep increase from Social Class V to Social Class I in the proportion obtaining privately paid help and yet there is also a slight increase in the proportion feeling the need for someone to help with the housework. In studying this table, it should be remembered that nearly a third of those getting help from the local council were making some payment for it.

TABLE 16

Percentage of persons of different social class who were receiving public or private domestic help, or who said help was needed; Britain 1962

Source of domestic help	Social Class					
	I	II	III non-manual	III manual	IV	V
	%	%	%	%	%	%
Local authority ...	1	2	4	6	4	4
Privately paid ...	42	27	12	5	3	2
Other (e.g. family) or none, but need felt	10	7	6	6	6	4
Other (e.g. family) or none, no need felt	47	64	78	83	87	90
Total	100	100	100	100	100	100
Number	81	555	396	1,188	1,033	447

Note: 42 persons were classed in armed services occupations, and 10 had had no occupation. Another 315 were unclassifiable (90 on the source of domestic help, and 225 on social class).

There is considerable prima facie evidence, therefore, that most at least of those feeling a need for domestic help have severe physical or social difficulties and might qualify for council help if it were available. Even if some of them do not qualify for help, there is reason for assuming that some other old people who say they do not need help have serious difficulties and ought to be offered it. For example,

1. As defined by the Registrar-General.

there were 31 men and 158 women in the sample, totalling 189, who said at another point in the interview that they could not undertake heavy housework, or could do so only with difficulty, *and* who said they had no help at all—whether from relatives, friends, council or paid domestics. Yet they also said they did not need anyone to help. They accounted for 4·6 per cent of the sample (representing another 268,000 in the elderly population). It is more than likely that some of them, and perhaps others who have insufficient help from family or friends, would qualify for assistance from local councils, if such assistance were offered and if they could be persuaded to accept it. Scrutiny of our interview schedules suggested that many old people are reluctant to admit the need for help. Some are old women who stubbornly try to discount or overcome infirmity.

Mrs Alfington is a widow of 81 living alone near a small town in Kent. She is housebound and suffers badly from rheumatism. "If I drop anything I can't pick it up". There are several personal and household functions she cannot perform and she is severely incapacitated. A son and a daughter live a few minutes walk away but appear to see her only at weekends. Her daughter "bought me slippers and brought me dinner on Sunday". When asked about someone to help with the housework, she answered " I don't want anyone. I manage somehow".

Some are men who appear to need help even though they remain active.

Mr Hoodgold is a widower of 76 who lives alone in a terraced house in a Lancashire cotton town. The front door opens directly into the living room. The grate is full of ash and bits of paper and there is dust everywhere, covering the rickety furniture, ancient radios, old pipes and odd bits of clothing. The kitchen is an improvised outhouse. The windows are thick with grime and one, which is broken, is boarded up. Mr Hoodgold is extraordinarily agile and showed me how he can touch his feet with his palms, keeping his legs straight. He goes for long walks and swims once a week. He has had three wives, from two of whom he separated, and this may partly account for his poor relations with two sons and two daughters born from the three marriages. One of the children is in London but he sees little of the three who live in Oldham. "They were most attached to their mothers". He is frightened only of going into hospital and losing his home. He didn't want meals or home help services. "I'd rather do it myself". But plainly the housework isn't done.

These examples suggest something of the diversity of the problems experienced by old people and the diversity of the resources they have to overcome them. They also suggest how difficult it may sometimes be to determine eligibility for help. But any estimate of unmet need made on the basis of the expressed desire for help on the part of old people is, in the final analysis, likely to be much too low.

Table 17 shows how often those who did have aid were being visited by a council home help. The great majority were visited on only one or two days a week. Compared with old people paying privately for domestic help, significantly fewer (less than 13 per cent compared with 24 per cent) received help on four or more days per week. Some of those who were given considerable help would otherwise have had to enter a hospital or residential Home.

Mrs Hoake is a widow of 70 who lives alone in a small flat on the first floor of a house in Glasgow. She is a diabetic, almost blind, cannot walk and has had several operations in the last few years, spending a total of 49 nights in hospital in the last twelve months. By our criteria she is very severely incapacitated. She sees her general practitioner every month or so. A home help from the local council comes seven days of the week to clean, light fires, cook, and make her bed. She leaves tea in a vacuum flask when she goes. Mrs Hoake's son and daughter both live in Canada and write every few weeks. One sister living nearby and a neighbour call most days. The interviewer noted: "she has to sit about all day. Bears her disability very well. Just says there is no use in grumbling. Was very glad I called. Said it passed the time. Said the National Assistance Board was very kind to her but doesn't understand she has to pay the home help 14s. of her money (from national assistance) every week".

TABLE 17

Percentage of old people getting home help once or more times a week from the local authority; Britain 1962

	Per cent of old people visited by a	
Number of days visited in week	Local authority home help	Private domestic help
	%	%
One	34	42
Two	37	22
Three	16	11
Four or more	13	24
Total	100	100
Number	167	337

Note: Unclassifiable, 5 persons receiving local authority help and 30 persons receiving private domestic help.

We did not ask whether old people wanted aid more frequently but evidence from local studies suggests that a minimum rather than an adequate service is often provided. Restrictions are placed on the kind of work a home help undertakes and a visit once or twice a week is insufficient to deal with needs which may arise daily, such as lighting fires, shopping and changing linen. Miss Sainsbury and her colleagues found that in Fulham those getting home help still had major un-fulfilled needs—and not only at weekends.[1] A few years ago Dr Boucher gave some vivid examples in a semi-official report of the extreme variation in the service in different parts of England and Wales.[2] Judging from the latest annual reports of the Ministry of Health and the plans of the local authorities the variation in service is still as wide. According to the revised ten-year plans of the local authorities for health and welfare published in July 1964, Oldham, for example, has three or four times as many home helps per 1,000 population as Manchester, Cheshire, Liverpool and Bootle. The projection of the plans to 1974 suggests that differences of this order for many areas of the country will remain.[3] We know of no evidence of local variations in need to justify differences in services of this magnitude.

The mobile meals service

We have already noted that just over 1 per cent of the sample received a cooked meal at least once a week from the mobile meals services—many of whom were incapacitated and lived alone. All other old people were asked whether they would like to receive them. As many as 5·9 per cent of both men and women said they would. They represented approximately 344,000 old persons in the population. This means that there are more than five times as many old people in Britain saying they would like to have a meal brought by the mobile meals services as there are old people actually receiving this service.

> Mrs Prothergast is a widow of 78 living with her brother of 75 in a dormitory suburb of London. She cannot climb stairs and is very severely incapacitated, being out of hospital only a few weeks. Her leg is bandaged from the thigh down and she is in constant pain. Although she has drugs to sleep at night she tries to avoid taking them in the day because they make her feel so awful. She sits in a chair most of the day and although her brother does what he can and a friend comes in to help with the housework every day, she feels the need for help. "I seem to have no strength to do anything". She said she could only afford half a pint of milk each day and would like more money for coal and food. She would like to have hot meals delivered.

But do all these people really mean it? And is there other evidence that they need such a service? As with the home help service it is possible only to answer these questions in part. These old people numbered 235 in both stages of the 1962 survey. Significantly more of them than of the rest of the sample were bedfast or severely

1. Sainsbury, S., "Home Services for the Aged", *New Society*, 2nd April, 1964.
2. Boucher, C., *Survey of Services Available to the Chronic Sick and Elderly*, 1954–5, Reports on Public Health and Medical Subjects, No. 98, London, HMSO, 1957.
3. *Health and Welfare: The Development of Community Care*, London, HMSO, July 1964.

49

incapacitated, living alone and childless or, if they had children, were separated from those they had. Table 18 shows some of their characteristics. Perhaps the most telling statement is that among the 4,000 people interviewed there were more than twice as many moderately or severely incapacitated people living alone saying they wanted meals (55) as there were receiving them (21).

TABLE 18

Percentage of persons saying they would and would not like cooked meals brought by the "Meals on Wheels" service who had certain characteristics; Britain 1962

Characteristics	Per cent of old people wanting meals delivered	Per cent of old people not wanting meals delivered
Total number	235	3,710
	%	%
Severely incapacitated (including bedfast)	18	7
Moderately incapacitated	33	24
Living alone	46	20
Childless	26	24
Has children, but neither children nor other relatives live at home or within ten minutes journey*	36	27

Note: 46 having meals from the mobile meals service are excluded. Unclassifiable, 76.
* Percentage of those with children.

Just as it might nonetheless be argued that *some* of these old people may not have 'needed' meals to be delivered, so it might also be argued that others needed them but would not say they wanted them. We found that there were 31 people, or nearly 1 per cent of the sample, who said they could not prepare a hot meal or had difficulty in doing so and who also said they had no-one to help them, but who did not want meals delivered. Although further research should be carried out our provisional conclusion must stand: there is prima facie evidence for a five-fold expansion of this service. This conclusion is broadly supported by the only detailed survey of mobile meals services that has been carried out.[1] Moreover, the estimate of future scope for expansion seems to be a conservative one. No account was taken in our survey of persons receiving one, two or three meals a week who felt the need for more[2]—though spontaneous remarks were sometimes made to this effect.

Mrs Thwaite lives alone, is housebound and gets meals on Wednesdays and Fridays. She would like them every day. One of her hands is paralysed and she can cook only with great difficulty. She often has a banana for breakfast and on days other than Wednesdays and Fridays, she makes herself bacon and egg, tea and bread in the afternoon and biscuits and cheese at night.

---

1   Harris, A., *Meals on Wheels for Old People*, London, the Government Social Survey, for the National Corporation for the Care of Old People, 1961.
2. Miss Harris presented convincing evidence for expansion in this sense. *Ibid*, p. 46.

A fifth of those receiving meals received them only on one day, and another half only on two days, a week. The remaining third received them on three, four or five days a week.

Chiropody

Before 1959 the organisation of chiropody services was not a statutory responsibility and local authorities were restricted to supporting voluntary associations. From April 1959 the Minister allowed local councils to develop such services among their responsibilities for the prevention of illness under the National Health Service Act.[1] Nearly all local authorities provided a service by 1962, most of them directly but some through a voluntary association.[2] Most schemes now provide treatment in local authority clinics and some in the private surgeries of chiropodists, but these clinics and surgeries are often far apart and domiciliary visits tend to be infrequent, in some areas none being paid.

Seven per cent of the old people in the sample were receiving chiropody treatment regularly through a public or voluntary service. Nearly half of these, or 3·2 per cent, paid some part of the cost. Another 11 per cent paid privately for treatment. There were yet another 11½ per cent who felt the need for treatment regularly.[3] This percentage represents approximately 670,000 persons in the elderly population of Britain, as Table 19 shows.

TABLE 19

Percentage of old persons having and feeling the need for chiropody treatment; Britain 1962

Source of chiropody treatment	Men	Women	Men and women	
	%	%	%	Estimated number in private households—Britain
Having chiropody, public or voluntary	5·0	8·9	7·3	425,000
Having chiropody, privately paid	5·3	15·4	11·3	658,000
No chiropody, need felt ...	9·2	13·0	11·5	670,000
No chiropody, no need felt ...	80·5	62·7	69·9	4,072,000
Total	100·0	100·0	100·0	5,825,000
Number	1,623	2,423	4,046	—

Note: Unclassifiable, 21. A number of those not having chiropody treatment were, of course, receiving unskilled help from relatives and others. All population estimates are subject to sampling error (Appendix 2).

1. Under Section 28, Prevention of Illness, Care and After-Care, of the National Health Service Act of 1946. The LCC and Essex County Council established chiropody services before the introduction of the National Health Service.
2. In 1962 chiropodists obtained State Registration under the terms of the Professions Supplementary to Medicine Act, 1960.
3. The question was: "Do you need someone to see to your feet regularly?"

Those depending for treatment on a public or voluntary service numbered 297 in the sample. As many as 59 per cent of them were moderately or severely incapacitated and 35 per cent lived alone (43 per cent of women, compared with 13 per cent of men, lived alone). Another 33 per cent lived only with a husband or wife.

In the survey we sought to apply a simple index of whether or not old people could care for their feet and adopted the question "can you cut your own toe-nails without difficulty?" Sixty-seven per cent of the entire sample had no difficulty, but 16 per cent found the function difficult and a further 17 per cent said they could not do it at all. The last group numbered 690 and as many as 76 per cent of them received no professional treatment.

Table 20 shows the results of relating ability to cut toe-nails to the receipt of or demand for treatment. More than three-quarters of old people having free or subsidised treatment were unable to cut their toe-nails or had difficulty in doing so. Rather more than half those paying privately for treatment, but over three-fifths of those not receiving but feeling a need for treatment, were similarly handicapped. There were significantly more persons experiencing difficulty in each of these three categories than among old people neither receiving nor wanting treatment.

TABLE 20

Percentage of old persons having and not having chiropody treatment who had difficulty in caring for their feet; Britain 1962

Whether able to cut toe-nails	Having chiropody		No chiropody	
	Public or voluntary service	Privately paid	Need felt	No need felt
	%	%	%	%
No	57	38	29	8
Yes, with difficulty	19	19	33	13
Yes, without difficulty	24	43	38	79
Total	100	100	100	100
Number	294	460	448	2,795

Note: Unclassifiable, 70 (including 48 bedfast).

Fewer proportionately of those not getting but feeling the need for treatment than of those actually receiving free or subsidised treatment said they were unable to cut their own toe-nails. But two other matters should also be noted. The group as a whole was proportionately half as many again in number. Also, rather more than half the persons saying they needed treatment regularly told us that they had no other source of help, not even the unskilled services of a relative or friend.

It is possible to present many different analyses of our data. But perhaps the most important fact is that among the most incapacitated old people in Britain there are more than twice as many saying they need help from the public social services as are receiving it. Table 21 picks out housebound persons having difficulty in caring for their feet, for example, and compares them with the mobile in an equivalent condition. Twenty per cent of the latter, compared with 10 per cent of the former, were receiving treatment from public and voluntary services. Despite their immobility significantly fewer of the housebound received treatment. Slightly more of them were not having treatment, but felt the need for it. The housebound find difficulties in getting taken to treatment centres and in many areas of the country there are no opportunities of receiving treatment at home. The data are rather disturbing and seem to call for an inquiry to find whether there should be an overhaul of existing methods of administering services.[1]

TABLE 21

Percentage of housebound and of mobile old persons having difficulty in caring for their feet who receive chiropody treatment; Britain 1962

Source of chiropody treatment	Old persons who find it difficult or are unable to cut toe-nails	
	Housebound	Mobile
	%	%
Having chiropody, public or voluntary ...	10	20
Having chiropody, privately paid ...	16	22
No chiropody, need felt	23	19
No chiropody, no need felt	51	39
Total	100	100
Number	311	828

Note: Unclassifiable, 1 housebound person.

Other deficiencies in the present development of chiropody services are revealed when utilisation and unfulfilled need or demand are related to social class. Table 22 shows that rather more of Social Classes I and II than of Social Classes III, IV and V already have professional treatment from private, voluntary and public sources, and that rather fewer of them not receiving such treatment feel the need for it.

There is a further approach to the question of unmet need. Among the old people who said they did not require regular foot

---

1. At the time of writing the data collected during the survey of residential institutions and hospitals had not been analysed but a first scrutiny showed that nearly half of the elderly residents and patients were not having chiropody treatment (including attention from nursing staff) regularly.

TABLE 22
Percentage of old persons of different social class who receive or feel the need for chiropody treatment; Britain 1962

Source of chiropody treatment	Social Class					
	I	II	III non-manual	III manual	IV	V
	%	%	%	%	%	%
Public or voluntary service	2	6	6	9	8	8
Privately paid ...	20	18	14	8	9	8
Non-professional or none, need felt ...	6	8	13	11	13	10
Non-professional or none, no need felt	72	68	67	72	71	74
Total	100	100	100	100	100	100
Number	82	557	396	1,193	1,040	457

Note: A further 42 persons were classed in armed services occupations, 10 had no occupation and 290 were unclassifiable.

treatment, there were 248, or 6·1 per cent of the sample, who not only admitted they were unable to cut their toe-nails or had difficulty in doing so, but said they had no other source of help (a third of them were living entirely alone). They represent 355,000 old persons in the population. It is likely that a large number of them might benefit from an extended chiropody service, if they could be persuaded to have treatment.

We did not investigate old people's experiences of public and private treatment and whether or not they found it adequate. But the evidence we have produced of large minorities of the elderly population obtaining and seeking treatment in some form and the large proportion experiencing trouble with their feet and toe-nails raises important questions about the size and achievements of the service. It seems that many more people need treatment. This is a conclusion reached in many local studies, including some depending on careful medical examinations.[1] There is a very sharp difference indeed according to social class in the proportions having and demanding treatment. Moreover, the relative neglect of the housebound may, in part, explain their immobility.

Perhaps the crucial question is whether routine professional examination if not treatment should complement unskilled care of old people's feet. Unskilled services performed by a husband or wife, a daughter or another relative or a friend should perhaps no longer be accepted as adequate care for the elderly, at least for those who are

1. For example, in a recently published report of a survey of old people in Edinburgh, in which a random sample were medically examined, 43 per cent had disabilities of the feet and the authors concluded "clearly a more effective chiropody service is needed". Williamson, J., *et al.*, "Old People at Home: Their Unreported Needs", *The Lancet*, 23rd May 1964. For an earlier example, see Hobson, J., and Pemberton, J., *The Health of the Elderly at Home*, London, Butterworth, 1955.

already infirm.   Good standards of foot care are basic to many other services for the elderly.   The Society of Chiropodists takes the view that a chiropody service for the aged in particular is vital "since the maintenance of mobility and independence are cardinal aims in geriatric medicine.   Proper chiropodial treatment can literally keep many old people 'on their feet' . . .".[1]   Foot conditions affect almost all activities—getting about inside and outside the house, climbing and descending stairs and even standing to prepare and cook a hot meal.   While professional chiropody is at present the prerogative of a minority it may be a service which all old people, and particularly those in their late seventies and eighties, should enjoy.   Its 'preventive' functions may come to be regarded as seriously as preventive dental care.

Hearing aid services

Poor hearing is another common handicap in old age which restricts communication and utilisation of social services.   During the survey old people were asked whether they had difficulty in hearing an ordinary conversation even with a hearing aid.   Table 23 shows that a third of the sample admitted or were observed to have a little or a lot of difficulty.[2]   More men than women had difficulty.

TABLE 23

Percentage of old persons who had difficulty in hearing; Britain 1962

Degree of difficulty with hearing	Men	Women	Men and women
	%	%	%
A lot	8	6	6
A little	25	23	24
None admitted, but observed	4	3	3
None	63	68	66
Total	100	100	100
Number	626	941	1,567

Note: This table and others on hearing are based only on questions asked in the second stage of the survey.

However, only 6·3 per cent of the sample (representing 367,000 persons in the population) possessed a hearing aid (nearly 5 per cent had a National Health Service aid and nearly 2 per cent a private aid) and half of them said they did not use the aid regularly.   In view of the numbers experiencing difficulty with their hearing these figures

1.   "Memorandum on Chiropody in the National Health Service", in *The Chiropodist*, Vol. 19, July 1964, p. 144.
2.   It should also be noted that 21 persons in the sample (or just over 1 per cent) said they had no difficulty in hearing, and we observed none, but nonetheless said they had a hearing aid.   Perhaps they had used it in earlier years when their hearing had been faulty or had been thought to be faulty.

are surprising, and disturbing. Table 24 shows that even among those who had a lot of difficulty with their hearing only 34 per cent possessed an aid, including only 11 per cent who used one regularly.

TABLE 24

Percentage of old persons having different degrees of difficulty in hearing who used an aid regularly; Britain 1962

Whether possessing and using an aid	Degree of difficulty in hearing			
	A lot	A little	None admitted but observed	None
	%	%	%	%
Aid—used regularly	11	6	10	1
Aid—not used regularly ...	25	4	8	1
No aid	66	90	84	98
Total	102	100	102	100
Number	100	376	51	1,038
Replies	102	378	52	1,038

Note: Unclassifiable, 2.   Regular use defined as daily use.   A few persons gave two replies because they had two aids.

While some persons with hearing loss cannot benefit from an aid expert opinion is unanimous in holding that the great majority can be helped.   But a real problem is the difficulty for infirm people of manipulating the NHS aid, particularly if it is one of the old battery models, rather than one of the more recent transistor models.   Moreover, both those who have and those who might qualify for the NHS aid know that it is more unsightly and more cumbersome than most commercial products.[1]   It is not easy to obtain domiciliary examinations from trained otologists under the National Health Service and routine examinations are only provided in some experimental clinics and by some progressive general practitioners.   The present system is based on self-reporting of condition and this has many drawbacks, as a number of studies have shown.   General practitioners tend to accept hearing loss in old people without encouraging an examination and sometimes are not aware of its existence.[2]

The information supplied about aural examinations by the sample raises further misgivings.   A large number of those with hearing difficulties had never had an aural examination and a further large number not for more than five years—whether by a consultant, a general practitioner or even a district nurse.   Table 25 shows that nearly half of those without a hearing aid who had difficulty in hearing had never had their ears examined and over a fifth not for more than

1.   For an excellent discussion of the advantages and disadvantages of the Medresco aid, and of recent developments in services for the deaf, see Gregory, P., *Deafness and Public Responsibility* Welwyn, Codicote Press, 1964.
2.   Williamson, J., *et al.*, "Old People at Home: Their Unreported Needs", *op. cit.*

five years. Even among those with a hearing aid more than a quarter had not been examined for more than five years.[1] Among those with severe hearing difficulty nearly one third (31 per cent) had never had an aural examination and a further quarter not for more than five years.

TABLE 25

Percentage of old people with hearing difficulty whose hearing had been examined recently; Britain 1962

Last aural examination	Old people with a hearing aid	Old people without an aid who had difficulty in hearing	All with an aid or difficulty in hearing
	%	%	%
Never	5	48	41
More than 5 years previously	23	23	23
3–5 years previously ...	20	8	10
Less than 3 years previously...	53	21	26
Total	100	100	100
Number ... ... ·...	97	447	544

Note: Unclassifiable, 4.

As with some other subjects investigated in this national survey, we would not claim to have obtained nearly as much information on the problem of deafness as deserves to be collected. The extent to which hearing loss limits social communication, the relation of deafness to mental impairment (or the appearance of mental impairment), why so many old people do not use their hearing aids, and why so many with hearing loss do not even have an aid—all these are matters for intensive inquiry. But, taken with the results of a recent study of deafness,[2] our data amount to *prima facie* evidence of deficiency on a scale to justify national concern and inquiry. Nearly two-thirds of those with difficulty in hearing had never had an aural examination or had not had an examination for more than five years. They represented 22·3 per cent of the total sample or nearly 1,300,000 persons in the elderly population. Even if we discount those with slight or moderate hearing loss, 210,000 with severe difficulty remain. Moreover, there appear to be approximately 255,000 old people in Britain with severe hearing loss who do not have a hearing aid and another 93,000 who have an aid but do not use it regularly.

Hearing difficulties of persons in hospitals and other institutions

The proportion of the elderly population living in hospitals and other institutions who had difficulty in hearing was larger than of the elderly population living at home. Table 26 shows that 12 per

---

1.   In the survey of institutions it was not possible to collect complete data but of those with a hearing aid even fewer (less than a third) had had an aural examination within the previous three years.
2.   Gregory, P., *op. cit.*

cent had severe hearing difficulty and another 30 per cent some difficulty.

TABLE 26
Percentage of old persons in hospitals and other institutions who had difficulty in hearing; Britain 1963

(sub-sample of 1,102 in institutions)

Degree of difficulty with hearing	Men	Women	Men and women
	%	%	%
A lot	12	12	12
A little	23	17	18
None admitted, but observed ...	14	11	12
None	51	60	58
Total	100	100	100
Number	322	768	1,090

Note: Unclassifiable, 12.

However, the proportion possessing a hearing aid was only 7·2 per cent (compared with 6·3 per cent) and therefore there were considerably more old people in the institutional population with difficulty in hearing who did not have an aid. And rather fewer of those with an aid used it regularly (two-fifths compared with half). We also found that these results were not attributable to the higher proportion of the institutional sample who were considered to be mentally impaired. The data, again, provide a strong *prima facie* case for national inquiry. The problems of communication between, and rehabilitation of, the elderly in institutions may be aggravated by insufficient use of modern aids.

Ophthalmic services

Proportionately more old people in the sample living at home had had an examination of the eyes than of the ears within the previous three years—52 per cent compared with 27 per cent. But 24 per cent had never been examined or had not been examined for more than five years. They represent approximately 1,316,000 old persons in the population. Discounting those with little or no difficulty in seeing, there were 5·6 per cent of the entire sample who had severe difficulty in seeing and who possessed spectacles but said they had never had an examination of the eyes or had not had one for more than five years. They represent approximately 326,000 persons in the population. There seems to be some reason for investigating how and why this can happen and whether the present system needs overhaul.[1]

1. Some local studies have concluded that there is a need for reform. For example, the latest of these notes "that the procedure for obtaining and changing spectacles and having an examination of the eyes is somewhat cumbersome and acting as a deterrent to many old people in having regular examination of the eyes. We would favour setting up a special ophthalmic clinic for the elderly as is done in the case of those requiring chiropody". Bamlett, R., and Milligan, H. C., "Health and Welfare Services for the Over 75's: A Geriatric Survey at West Hartlepool" *The Medical Officer*, 21st June, 1963.

There were some old people in the sample who used spectacles bought years before in a chain store or passed on from a relative or friend and they were among the few (4 per cent) who had never been examined by an oculist, optician or general practitioner. Only a small minority of the old people did not have spectacles, as Table 27 shows. But roughly a third of them had a lot of or some difficulty in seeing, which, together with our other evidence, suggests that more might be done to ensure that old people have regular eyesight examinations.

TABLE 27

Percentage of old persons with and without spectacles who had difficulty in seeing; Britain 1962

Degree of difficulty in seeing	Men	Women	Men and women
	%	%	%
Registered blind	0·5	0·2	0·4 } 1·2
Registered partially sighted	1·3	0·5	0·8 }
Without Spectacles			
Having a lot of difficulty in seeing ...	0·0	0·5	0·3 }
Having some difficulty in seeing ...	1·4	0·9	1·1 } 4·2
Having no difficulty	3·2	2·6	2·8 }
With Spectacles			
Having a lot of difficulty in seeing ...	4·0	9·8	7·5 }
Having some difficulty in seeing ...	18·9	23·0	21·4 } 94·7
Having no difficulty	70·7	62·5	65·8 }
Total	100·0	100·0	100·0
Number	624	939	1,563

Note: This table is based on the sample interviewed in Stage II of the survey, numbering 1,567. Un-classifiable, 4.

The total of 1·2 per cent who were registered blind or partially sighted, representing 70,000 persons in the population, may be slightly below the true figure.[1] The table also shows that with or without spectacles another 8 per cent (representing 454,000) had a lot of difficulty in seeing. While we did not obtain more details about their difficulties we felt there were some at least who might be placed on the local authority registers of the partially sighted so that they might be visited and considered for special services. Altogether the extension of local authority work for persons with various disabilities seemed to be urgent.

Ophthalmic services in hospitals and other institutions

Rather more old people in institutions than at home had difficulty in seeing. Five per cent were blind. A total of 17 per cent were blind or had a lot of difficulty in seeing, compared with 9 per cent of the elderly population in private households. But if Table 28 is compared with Table 27, it can be seen that considerably fewer among the institutional population, 72 per cent compared with 95 per cent,

---

1. In 1962 there were 80,716 registered blind and partially sighted persons aged 65 and over in England and Wales. *Report of the Ministry of Health for the Year Ended 31st December* 1963 Cmnd 2389, London, HMSO, 1964, p. 116.

had spectacles. Those without spectacles included a large minority who had some or a lot of difficulty in seeing. This finding deserves to be treated with concern. Although it may be difficult or unsafe sometimes for mentally confused or frail old people to wear spectacles the loss of them can foster insecurity and confusion. Too often it seems to be regarded as administratively convenient for old people to be deprived of fragile aids. Too many staff excuse such deprivation on grounds that the aids can get broken or lost.

TABLE 28

Percentage of old persons with and without spectacles in institutions who had difficulty in seeing; Britain 1963

(sub-sample of 1,102 in institutions)

Degree of difficulty in seeing	Men	Women	Men and women
	%	%	%
Blind	1·9	5·8	4·6
Without spectacles			
Having a lot of difficulty in seeing ...	3·1	2·0	2·3
Having some difficulty in seeing ...	6·6	3·6	4·5
Having no difficulty	17·5	15·9	16·4
With spectacles			
Having a lot of difficulty in seeing ...	10·3	9·5	9·8
Having some difficulty in seeing ...	18·8	21·7	20·8
Having no difficulty	41·7	41·4	41·5
Total	100·0	100·0	100·0
Number	319	755	1,074

Frequency of medical care

Almost all the sample were registered with a general practitioner in the National Health Service. As Table 29 shows, slightly fewer than 2 per cent were not registered with a doctor in the National Health Service and paid privately for medical care—representing about 110,000 old people in Britain. Scarcely any claimed they had no doctor.

We were unable to collect detailed information about medical consultations but Table 30 shows when the old people in the sample had last seen their doctors. More than one in eight had seen a doctor within the previous week. Rather more women than men had seen a doctor recently, but between a quarter and a third of both sexes had not seen one for more than a year. The percentages correspond closely with the results of a special survey of 100 general practices in England and Wales in 1955–6.[1] We found that more old people

---

1. In that year 68 per 100 male patients and 73 per 100 female patients aged 65 and over had consulted their doctors. Table 30 below shows that among our sample 68 men and 71 women in every 100 said they had seen their doctors during the previous year. Logan, W. P. D., and Cushion, A. A., *Morbidity Statistics from General Practice*, Vol. 1, London, HMSO, 1958, p. 27.

TABLE 29
Percentage of old persons having a doctor in the National Health Service; Britain 1962

Whether doctor in NHS	Men	Women	Men and women
	%	%	%
National Health Service	97·9	98·0	98·0
Privately paid	1·7	1·9	1·9
No doctor	0·4	0·0	0·2
Total	100·0	100·0	100·0
Number	1,620	2,400	4,020

Note: Unclassifiable, 47.

in their eighties than in their late sixties had seen a doctor recently, as one would expect, but the increase with age was not as pronounced for women as for men. Forty-three per cent of men, and 40 per cent of women aged 80 and over, had seen a doctor within the previous month, compared with 21 per cent and 35 per cent respectively of those aged 65 to 69.

TABLE 30

Percentage of old persons seeing a doctor within different previous periods; Britain 1962

When last seeing a doctor	Men	Women	Men and women
	%	%	%
Within last week	11·5	14·0	13·0
Over a week and not more than a month previously	19·4	21·5	20·7
Over a month, not more than three months previously	15·0	15·3	15·2
Over 3 months, not more than a year previously	22·2	20·4	21·1
More than a year previously	31·9	28·7	30·0
Total	100·0	100·0	100·0
Number	1,615	2,408	4,023

Note: Unclassifiable, 44.

Those old persons who lived in residential institutions and Homes were also asked how recently they had seen a doctor. Somewhat surprisingly, as Table 31 shows, the proportion seeing a doctor within the previous week and within the previous month were only slightly larger than of the elderly population at home and as many as 18 per cent said that it was more than a year since they had seen a doctor. Routine medical examinations appear to have been introduced by only a small number of local authorities.

TABLE 31

Percentage of old persons in residential institutions and at home who had seen a doctor within different previous periods; Britain 1962-1963

When last seeing a doctor	Living in residential institutions	Living at home
	%	%
Within last week	14·4	13·0
Over a week and not more than a month previously	27·7	20·7
Over a month, not more than three months previously	19·3	15·2
Over three months, not more than a year previously	20·3	21·1
More than a year previously	18·3	30·0
Total	100·0	100·0
Number	404	4,023

Note: Unclassifiable, 74 and 44 respectively.

All old people (with the exception of those in hospitals) were also asked whether they saw their doctors as often as they wanted. The great majority said they did but of those living at home 3·5 per cent (2·8 per cent of men and 4·0 per cent of women) said they did not. Significantly more of those living in residential institutions, 9·4 per cent, said they did not. Altogether they represent 214,000 persons in the elderly population. Table 32 shows that most of those who wanted to see more of a doctor had not seen one during the previous month. More than half of those living at home and rather less than half of those living in residential institutions had not seen one during the previous three months. They were not people, therefore, who were already taking up an exceptional amount of doctors' time. They were usually people who sought attention for some chronic ailment; over half of those living at home were moderately or severely incapacitated and 10 per cent had been ill in hospital during the previous twelve months.

It would, of course, be wrong to read too much into the answers to a single question, without more elaborate inquiry. The volume of complaint from old people, it should be noted, is small. Yet the volume of unreported and otherwise unknown illness and disability is, to judge from several recent medical inquiries, very much larger. Among different elderly populations a high prevalence of morbidity and disability has been found which is not being treated at all or not being treated adequately—malnutrition, anaemia, locomotion and foot disabilities, dementia, deafness, poor sight, bad teeth and so on.[1] The recent report by a Committee of the Royal College of Physicians on *The Care of the Elderly in Scotland* concluded "we are convinced

---

1. Williamson, J., *et al.*, *op. cit.*; Richardson, I. M., *op. cit*; Edge, J. R. and Nelson, I. D. M., "Survey of Arrangements for the Elderly in Barrow-in-Furness, 1 and 2", *Medical Care*, October–December, 1963, and January–March, 1964.

TABLE 32
Percentage of old persons wanting and not wanting to see more of their doctors who had seen them within different previous periods; Britain 1962-1963

When last seeing a doctor	Whether feeling doctor seen sufficiently often			
	Yes		No	
	Living in residential institutions	Living at home	Living in residential institutions	Living at home
	%	%	%	%
Within last week	16	13	(3)	5
Over a week, not more than a month previously	28	21	(25)	15
Over a month, not more than three months previously ...	19	15	(28)	26
Over three months, not more than a year previously ...	19	21	(25)	28
More than a year previously ...	18	30	(19)	26
Total	100	100	100	100
Number	347	3,869	36	138

Note: Unclassifiable, 21 in residential institutions and 60 in private households. Bracketed figures indicate that the percentage is based on less than 50 replies.

that much avoidable discomfort and misery are commonplace". The demand for medical care is not the same thing as the need for medical care. We were struck by the diffidence of the persons in the sample when they spoke of their doctors. They did not wish to waste the time of busy men and women. One infirm woman said "He sees me often enough. His surgery is a long way and I don't like to bother him". And a man of 80, who lived with his wife of 75, said he didn't expect the doctor to call more often although "we would like to have a chance to explain. He never wants to know anything. He just writes a prescription or says 'I can't do anything about that' ". These were typical reactions.

Old people underestimated the seriousness of their condition, or were frightened of seeking advice, often because they did not want to admit difficulties which suggested loss of self-sufficiency and dependence on others. The real problem was not one of discouraging them from unnecessarily taking up the time of professional personnel, but of encouraging them, particularly those in urgent but unsuspected need, to use all the services and facilities available. The chief need appeared to be first, to find a method of organising routine medical examinations, particularly for the over-75's and those elderly patients discharged from hospital, and second, to persuade both the medical profession and the public not to accept ill-health and infirmity as necessary and inevitable features of old age.

Sheltered housing

In considering the services which help old people to live at home it is important not to overlook sheltered housing schemes that are now being developed. These schemes involve groups of dwellings which are specially designed—incorporating such features as handrails, non-slip floors, and shelves and cupboards which can be used without stooping or stretching. The dwellings are of several different types—self-contained bungalows, flats with separate bedrooms and sitting rooms, or flatlets comprising a bed-sitting-room with a bed recess and separate kitchen. Groups of bed-sitting rooms and flats usually have shared bathrooms and sometimes W.C.'s instead of having separate facilities for each dwelling. The distinguishing feature of the schemes is the housekeeper or warden to attend to any of the special needs of the old people in illness or infirmity. Usually a married woman lives with her family in a house at the corner of the cluster of bungalows or flatlets comprising the scheme. There are also certain communal facilities, such as a lounge with a TV set, a guest room and a wash-room. In many schemes there is a communicating bell system. According to the Ministry of Health there were six persons per 1,000 aged 65 and over in England and Wales in 1963 (totalling 35,000) who were accommodated in such schemes. The local authorities plan to increase this figure to 20 per 1,000 (totalling 113,000) by 1969.[1]

There is, however, immense variation in the provision of these special dwellings. A fifth of the County Boroughs and County Councils have yet to open any accommodation of this kind, while some councils, such as Barnsley and the housing authorities in the West Riding of Yorkshire, have already opened far more than the national average and still plan to expand far beyond the national rate in the next ten years.[2]

In fact, the country is only now beginning to awaken to the urgent need of special housing for the elderly. The first blue book outlining the local authorities' plans for health and welfare services, for example, was published in April 1963 and contained no precise reference to such housing. For a long time after the war priority was given to the needs of young families for homes and even when one-bedroom dwellings began to form a much higher proportion of the output of the local authorities this was at a time when their output formed a diminishing proportion of the housing built in Britain. In 1950 the councils built about two-thirds, and private builders about one third, of new houses, but by the late 1950s these proportions had been reversed. Thus the numbers of one-bedroom dwellings which were built by local authorities each year rose from about 17,000 to only 27,000 in the eight years between 1953 and 1960. It is probably fair to add that although the county borough, borough and district councils were made increasingly aware of the rising proportion of old people they were not properly informed about changes in the patterns

1. *Health and Welfare: The Development of Community Care*, London, HMSO, July, 1964.
2. In the West Riding of Yorkshire there are 29·1 special dwellings per 1,000 population aged 65 and over and the councils there propose increasing this figure to 97·4 by 1969. Barnsley had 17·9 per 1,000 in 1963 and proposes to have 88·5 by 1969. Dewsbury and Wakefield had just a few dwellings each in 1963 (1·2 and 4·3 per 1,000 respectively) and do not plan to open any more. *Ibid.*

of household relationships of old people—brought about by changes in the composition of the elderly population and also by the declining number of those reaching the pensionable ages who still had unmarried children living at home. It has been calculated that the number of households comprising one or two persons aged 65 and over is increasing by at least 40,000 a year.[1]

But does this mean that 40,000 new dwellings are needed for the elderly, and what proportion of the new dwellings should be sheltered dwellings? The answers to these questions depend on various kinds of information, including how many old people there are living at present in unsatisfactory accommodation which needs to be replaced; how many there are who live alone, who cannot or prefer not to live with their relatives or friends, and who are sufficiently infirm to require special housing and welfare services; and how many there are who live with others but for various reasons might prefer, or be advised, to live alone. The assumptions that will have to be explored before a final estimate can be reached are complex, and a first examination of our data allows us merely to suggest the scale of certain problems.

Poor housing is perhaps a bigger problem than has been appreciated. We asked about basic amenities—water, bath, kitchen and W.C. All but 5 per cent of the elderly people in the sample lived in a household with sole use of piped water and all but 8 per cent with sole use of a kitchen but 27 per cent did not have access to a bath and another 4 per cent shared a bath with another household. More important, 5 per cent (representing 291,000 in the population) did not have a W.C. and another 34 per cent (representing 1,980,000) only had access to a W.C. outside the house. Table 33 gives a simple measure of poor housing and shows how many old people lived in households lacking one or more of three basic facilities—sole use of fixed bath and kitchen and indoor W.C. As many as 6 per cent, representing 350,000 in the population, had none of the three, and another 22 per cent, representing 1,281,000 lacked two of them.

TABLE 33

Percentage of old persons having sole use of three basic housing amenities (bath, kitchen and indoors W.C.); Britain 1962

Number of amenities					Per cent of sample	Estimated number in total elderly population
					%	%
None	...	...	...	...	6·1	355,000
One	...	...	...	...	22·0	1,281,000
Two	...	...	...	...	15·5	903,000
Three	,,,	,,,	...	...	56·4	3,286,000
Total	...	...	...	...	100·0	5,825,000

Note: Estimates are of course subject to sampling error (Appendix 2).

1. Greve, J., *The Housing Problem*, Fabian Research Series 224, 1961, pp. 18–19.

Those living alone fared badly. Only 40 per cent had all three facilities; 14 per cent had none. Those living with married children fared better: 73 per cent having all three facilities and only 2 per cent none.

Again we found that a large number of old people preferred not to complain about the conditions in which they lived. Only two-fifths of those lacking all three basic facilities said there was something about the dwelling which they disliked or found inconvenient. Substantial proportions of those who did complain referred to bad design, lack of bathroom, too many stairs, the inconvenience of the W.C., the bad state of repair, cold and draughts and, interestingly, rooms that were too large. Many of them said they would like to move and certainly their need for good housing often overshadowed other needs.

Mr Shilwell is 80 and his wife 75. Both are frail and he has severe bronchitis. They rent two rooms on the ground floor of an old house in a Tyneside city which has no bathroom. The W.C. is in the back yard. They scarcely ever go out. He said "with my disability, it is becoming difficult to get to the front door. There's a long passage and two steps. And its very damp indeed". They very much want a modern ground-floor home with a bath and an indoor W.C. As for other needs, they are visited by a home help twice a week but "a bit more company would be nice. My eyes need testing but I can't get out. Not enough is done for people who are housebound. I don't like to ask for this and that all the time—just like charity".

Altogether 32 per cent of the sample (the proportion for each sex being roughly equal) said they would prefer to be in a different sort of dwelling, as Table 34 shows. Nearly half of them specifically mentioned a bungalow and nearly a third a *smaller* house or flat with fewer rooms. Small minorities referred to the need for modern plumbing and design, for privacy and for the elimination of stairs. Over half of them were prepared to move to obtain these advantages.

Table 34 suggests how conservative many old people are in their attitudes towards a change of dwelling or district. Over three-fifths wanted neither to have a different kind of dwelling nor to move to a different part of the same district or to a different district. As many as 85 per cent liked the district they were living in and another 9 per cent had no strong feelings either way. Only 6 per cent actively disliked it. When asked whether they wanted to move, however, 11 per cent said they wanted to move to another part of the same district, and 15 per cent to a new district entirely. Their attitude was partly determined by an awareness that suitable housing did not exist in their present district, or by a desire to follow married children to new housing in another district.

All those in the sample who lived alone (more than a fifth) were asked whether they preferred to carry on living alone. The vast majority, 91 per cent, said they did. Many of them saw members

TABLE 34

Percentage of old persons wanting a different kind of dwelling and wanting to move to a different district; Britain 1962

Attitude to dwelling and district	Men	Women	Men and women
	%	%	%
Wanting a different kind of dwelling and wanting to move to a different district	8	7	7 ⎫
Wanting a different kind of dwelling and wanting to move only to another part of the same district	5	7	6 ⎪
Wanting a different kind of dwelling and wanting to move either to a different district or to another part of the same district	4	3	3 ⎬ 32(2)
Wanting a different kind of dwelling but not wanting to move	15	16	15 ⎭
Not wanting a different kind of dwelling but wanting to move (1)	5	5	5
Neither wanting a different kind of dwelling nor wanting to move	63	61	62
Total	100	100	100
Number	980	1,448	2,428

Note: (1) To a different district or to another part of the same district.
(2) The discrepancy between the total and the sum of the sub-totals is due to rounding.
24 men and 48 women were unclassifiable.

of their families every day and exchanged services. Those who did not want to carry on living alone tended to be persons who saw less of children, and to be *younger* and *less* incapacitated. It may be that some of them had come to live alone early in retirement and could not reconcile themselves to a long period of life alone or still felt they could contribute to the running of a bigger household if they had the chance of moving into one. Similarly, those who lived with married children (11 per cent of the sample) were asked if they preferred to carry on living with them. Again, the vast majority (88 per cent) said they did—though some hesitated in their answers and made it plain that this was a realistic rather than an ideal choice. There are, of course, problems involved in exploring people's attitudes on such delicate questions and there were occasions when children were present during our interviews. Intensive interviewing would reveal that many persons make subtle qualifications to the attitudes they take. It is also true that many persons are aware of the lack of alternative housing, and that this affects their expressed preferences.

Can even a provisional figure be given of the number of old people who might, in time, live in sheltered housing? Perhaps an estimate might be based on the proportion of the persons in the sample who (a) lived entirely alone, (b) had no children living within ten minutes journey and (c) were moderately or severely incapacitated. There were 5·1 per cent, representing nearly 300,000 persons in the elderly population. This compares with the actual figure of 0·6 per cent in 1963 and the planned figure of 2·0 per cent in 1969. Although ours is a rough estimate it may be one which is rather too conservative. It does not include, for example, any infirm married couples who live on their own and who do not have children (or other relatives of a younger generation) living nearby. Their numbers are likely to be greater than the numbers of old people living entirely alone who are helped by the domiciliary services or by a paid domestic servant. Moreover, nearly half this group in the sample were living in housing which lacked at least one of the basic amenities about which information was collected—bath, kitchen and indoors W.C. Our conclusion must be that there is a very large deficiency of sheltered housing, quite apart from the separate deficiency of modern and well-designed housing for the elderly.

Do those receiving some community services need more?

We noted earlier that 11·8 per cent of the sample were receiving at least one domiciliary service. The total is 11·3 per cent for just three services—chiropody, home help and meals. Table 35 shows that most of the old people receiving these services received only one of them. Half those who received the meals service, 71 per cent of those getting home help and 86 per cent of those getting chiropody treatment received just the one service.

TABLE 35

Percentage of old people receiving home help, meals or chiropody services who received one or more of them; Britain 1962

Number of domiciliary services received	Men and women receiving home help, meals and chiropody services
	%
Three	0·9
Two	9·7
One	89·4
Total	100·0
Number	444

Note: A further 13 received at least one service, but were otherwise unclassifiable.

Further confirmation is needed of these important data, but it seems that the full resources of the community services may not be used by administrators and organisers of individual services. In some areas services are seen as *alternatives* rather than as complementing each other. One of the best possible checks on unmet need may be to organise reassessment of the services needed by old people already receiving one of them.

Summary

Much of the foregoing analysis has been concerned to reach provisional estimates of the extent to which certain community services for the aged might be expanded in the immediate future. One firm conclusion for policy is that substantially more old people than are receiving different services—sometimes double, treble, or quadruple the existing number—feel a need and otherwise seem to qualify for them. A second conclusion is that many of those receiving certain services —particularly the hearing aid, home help and meals services—are not getting all the help they might from the services in question; they need help more frequently, or the services need to be greatly improved and extended in scope. A third conclusion is that the services are not properly co-ordinated and many people receiving

TABLE 36

Summary of numbers in the elderly population requiring certain health and welfare services; Britain 1962

	Estimated number aged 65 and over
Total elderly population in private households	5,825,000
Home Help	
(i) Feeling a need for help with housework	332,000
(ii) Not feeling such need, but having difficulty with housework and having no one to help	268,000
Meals	
Expressing a wish for hot meals from the mobile meals service	344,000
Chiropody	
Feeling a need for someone to see to feet regularly ...	670,000
Hearing	
(i) Having *severe* difficulties in hearing but never having had an aural examination or none for more than 5 years	210,000
(ii) Having *severe* and *some* difficulties in hearing but never having had an aural examination or none for more than 5 years	1,300,000
(iii) Severe hearing loss but no aid ...	255,000
(iv) Severe hearing loss and having an aid, but not using it regularly	93,000
Sight	
(i) Severe difficulty in seeing, never having had an examination of the eyes or none for more than 5 years ...	326,000
(ii) Having severe difficulty in seeing, not registered with the local authority	454,000
Doctors	
(i) Living at home, wanting to see more of medical practitioner	204,000
(ii) Living in residential Homes, wanting to see more of medical practitioner	10,000
Special and Sheltered Housing	
(i) Lacking three basic amenities (indoor W.C. and sole use of bath and kitchen)	355,000
(ii) Lacking two of three basic amenities	1,281,000
(iii) Incapacitated and living alone and also no children living within ten minutes journey	297,000

Note: It must be emphasised that all estimates are subject to sampling error. See Appendix II.

only one service seem to need at least two or three services. These conclusions are not particularly new. A large number of local and regional studies have implied them for the country as a whole. But our data allow a number of national estimates to be made for the first time with some degree of confidence. These are summarised in Table 36 on the previous page and they make a daunting list. Some of the deficiencies in the Welfare State are larger than even the sternest critics have dared suggest. Not only is there strong evidence for a major expansion, in particular, of home help services, aids for disability and sheltered housing. There is also evidence that because of old people's diffidence total needs may have been underestimated. Some of our analyses by social class have suggested that needs are partly a function of expectations, and many old people are reluctant to confess their loss of independence or demand the services they appear to need. But there are indications, at least among middle and working-class people who are beginning to have contacts with professional services such as chiropody services, that the traditional reserve and tight-lipped self-sufficiency of old people in Britain is not nearly as rigid as it has been. There is greater readiness to see the social services as a means rather than as an obstacle to independence.

PART II

The Income and Assets of Older People

DOROTHY WEDDERBURN
(Department of Applied Economics,
University of Cambridge)

LIST OF TABLES

CHAPTER 4

A General Description of Financial Levels

The background to the study

In the introduction we described how, in the present study, we would examine the extent to which the social services were meeting the needs of elderly people, and how far these needs were themselves changing as a result of change in society itself. In Part I these problems were discussed in the context of the health and welfare services. In this part we shall study financial provision for old age in Britain today.

It might appear strange that, as western societies grow richer, academic interest in the problems of defining concepts such as financial need, poverty and minimum incomes should have revived.[1] Yet when Galbraith himself described an affluent society as one in which "wants are increasingly created by the process by which they are satisfied", such an interest was already heralded.[2] Definition of 'needs' cannot fail to be influenced by current standards of 'wants'; and it is clear that, whilst the British version of the affluent society may have solved the problem of poverty as it was known in this country in the 'thirties', it has also created new problems by raising levels of expectations. What then are contemporary financial 'needs'?

Politicians too, faced with competing claims upon their budgets have become increasingly interested in some concept of 'need' as a means of limiting a rising bill for social security benefits. In a debate at the end of 1963 the Government spokesman moved an amendment to the Opposition motion, which ended thus: "The Government will continue to improve benefits and in doing so will have regard particularly to those groups whose *need* is greatest" [our italics].

In the same debate the main speaker for the Opposition had referred to his Party's plans to "supplement the income of everybody who *needs* it"[3] [our italics]. Such views have been most often voiced in the discussions about pensions.

But before examining the meaning that can be given to such a notion as 'need' in the context of the financial problems of elderly people we must also ask what are the present levels of financial resources

---

1. See for instance Marshall, T. H., "The Affluent Society in Perspective" in *Sociology at the Cross Roads*, Heinemann, London, 1963.
2. Galbraith, J. K., *The Affluent Society*, Hamish Hamilton, London, 1958.
3   See for both speeches, *Hansard*, 10th December, 1963, Col. 248, Col. 243.

available to them? What is the contribution made to the income of older people by state provision of retirement pensions and national assistance? Is it possible to identify particular groups among people over retirement age whose income level is much lower than others? If so, who are they, and how large are such groups? These are some of the questions to which the material from the national survey of old people in Britain in 1962 enables us to attempt an answer.

The Government itself has not made a special survey of the income and expenditure of old people despite the extensive debate on pension policy which has been going on.[1] A start to providing some essential information about the financial circumstances of the old was made, however, in 1962, with the publication of the first results of a large-scale detailed study of the financial position of older people—the first to be carried out in this country since the war.[2] That report suggested that a far larger proportion of old people than had previously been realised derived all or nearly all of their income from the state, either as a retirement pension or as national assistance. It also showed that the most serious financial problems were those of single and widowed women. There has been reluctance in some quarters to accept some of these findings.[3] The size of sample was admittedly small,[4] and, perhaps more important, lack of finance had meant that the field-work was confined to seven areas. Although these were carefully chosen to be representative of the country as a whole, there is always the possibility that bias may arise with such a method. The present national survey is not open to such objections. The general method has already been described.[5] It is based on interviews with a multi-stage random national sample of individuals aged 65 and over, living in private households. To be meaningfully interpreted, however, the financial resources of a husband and wife must be treated as one. So in this discussion of income and savings the data relate to a sample of 3,146 'income units' contained within the sample of individuals.[6]

It is of considerable importance to find that the results of the national inquiry do, in fact, confirm and extend the conclusions of the

1. On 8th July 1964, the then Minister of Pensions, Mr Wood, announced that the Government would institute an inquiry into the number of people eligible but not applying for national assistance (*Hansard*, 9th July, 1964, Col. 586). That inquiry—restricted to people actually receiving a retirement pension—is now under way.

2. Cole, Dorothy with Utting, J., *The Economic Circumstances of Old People*, Codicote Press, Welwyn, 1962, The survey was generously supported by a grant from the Nuffield Foundation. Henceforth it will be referred to as the '1959–60 survey'. (See, too, the discussion of the 1959–60 survey in 'Poverty in Britain Today—The Evidence', Dorothy Cole Wedderburn, Vol. 10, *Sociological Review*, No. 3, 1962.)

3. See for instance discussion in *Hansard*, 30th January, 1962, Col. 892; 13th March, 1962, Col. 1148, 1165, etc.; 25th February, 1963, Col. 898; 9th July, 1964, Col. 578.

4. The published report is based on the analysis of material relating to 400 income units. The full sample is one of 1,046 income units.

5. See above, Introduction pp. 12–15.

6. There are three types of income unit: Men (that is single or widowed men aged 65 or over), Women (that is single or widowed women aged 65 or over), and Couples (that is a man and wife where the husband is aged 65 or over *irrespective* of the age of the wife). Since we felt that the husband's position was all important in determining the financial situation of a couple, cases of couples where the wife was 65 or over but married to a man under 65 have been excluded.

1959–60 survey. The main points to emerge may be summarised as follows:

(a) Income from the state is the most important single income source for the aged. For 7 out of 10 old people it is their main source of income. More than 3 in 10 have no income at all except that which they receive from the state. If income from non-state sources of less than £1 a week means that people can be described as 'primarily dependent' upon the state, then 5 out of every 10 old people are in this position.

(b) The main problem of very low or inadequate income is to be found among those old people who have ceased to work or, like older women, have never worked. The 10 per cent of old people who are in full-time employment remain at income levels much more nearly comparable with the general population.

(c) A significant group of old people, about 11 per cent, have incomes *lower* than appropriate national assistance scale rates, but do not receive national assistance. They are not all necessarily entitled to national assistance as the regulations stand. Certainly the economic position of this group requires attention.

(d) Single and widowed women emerge as the largest problem group among the aged. Although twice the proportion of women as of men and couples receive national assistance, the women still have lower incomes. True, the women are more likely to be sharing a home with other people; but often they share only with another woman, perhaps a widowed sister, or a single daughter—that is, people who themselves often have low incomes.

(e) Old people—men, women and couples alike—all tend to have lower incomes the older they are.

In what follows these conclusions will be explored in detail and the evidence to support them described. First, however, it is reasonable to ask how we can be sure that the survey results do give an accurate picture of the economic circumstances of the old.

Response and reliability; a comparison with official data

In the lay mind there is often considerable doubt about whether it is possible to collect reliable information about income and assets by survey method. Considerable progress has however been made in techniques for this kind of work in the last twenty years and government departments themselves use these methods.[1] There are two relevant questions. First, how representative is the co-operating sample? Second, how reliable is the information given by respondents?

1. For instance the 1955 Savings Survey by the Central Statistical Office, see Erritt, M. J. and Nicholson, J. L., "The 1955 Savings Survey", *Bulletin of the Oxford Institute of Statistics*, Vol. 20, 1958. The Ministry of Labour regularly collects details of family income in their continuing Family Expenditure Survey.

This survey started with a scientifically designed random sample but there were two kinds of non-response. In addition to the general non-response at the initial approach (both refusals and non-contacts) there were some individuals who having answered the first part of the questionnaire on health and welfare, refused to answer the financial questions. It is estimated that with these two forms of non-response combined there was failure to obtain co-operation from 20 per cent of all income units in the sample.[1] The financial data therefore are based upon information supplied by a total sample of 3,146 income units—495 men, 1,552 women and 1,099 couples. This sample of income units may be biassed from this non-response in ways which could have some bearing upon levels of financial resources.[2] There is probably some geographical bias in favour of the north; in favour of rural areas and in favour of areas of lower social status compared with areas of higher social status.[3] There may be some under-representation of women and over-representation of couples. But such differences between the co-operating and the total sample are small, and when the financial material is reweighted to correct for bias of these kinds it makes very little difference to the final estimate. If, for instance, the estimate of the proportions of income units who have no assets in each type of area are reweighted by the 'true' proportions in each type of area, the total proportion having no assets (36 per cent) remains unchanged.[4] It remains possible, of course, that the co-operating sample of income units within say, areas, is biassed in an upward or downward direction.

Another factor may affect the picture. The financial information obtained from these 3,146 income units was not, in every case, complete. Sometimes we know the amounts being received from one income source, but not from all sources. Such income units have been included in estimating the proportions receiving different kinds of income, but omitted from estimates of amounts. This extra-non-response affects another 207 income units or just under 5 per cent of the initial sample and these units are probably biassed towards the better-off. For instance we know that, as compared with those people for whom all amounts are known, more of these people are house-owners, have assets worth more than £500, and have employment and property income.

General experience of financial surveys leads one to expect that non-response will be heaviest among the better-off. But in surveys of the old one factor has to be set against this, which is the loss of information from the sick, the infirm and the mentally confused. This group may well contain a disproportionately large number of the

---

1. 'Estimated' because some assumptions have to be made about the number of income units in that part of the refusing sample where practically no information (particularly about marital status) is obtained.
2. See the discussion of non-response in the Introduction, p. 14.
3. As measured by the J-Index. See Gray, P. G., Corlett, T. and Jones, P., *The Proportion of Jurors as an Index of the Economic Status of a District*, Social Survey, London, 1951.
4. That is, 'true' as estimated from the distribution of the original sample co-operators and non-co-operators combined.

poorest. In the present survey, for instance, no financial information was obtained in the 116 cases of proxy interviews, accounting for about 15 per cent of the total number of incomplete cases.[1]

The information must also be assessed in relation to the effectiveness of the questionnaire in producing honest and reliable answers from those who did co-operate. The general method was one which has been used, with success, in a number of income surveys in this country. The only doubt concerns the asset information where the questions were confined to asking the respondent to indicate into which of a number of broad value groups his or her assets fell. It was known, when the survey was designed, that the absence of detailed prompting might lead to a certain amount of inaccuracy here, but this risk had to be run. The total length of interview could not be further extended without the possibility of reduced reliability as a result of the respondent's fatigue, and overall priority had to be given to the health and welfare aspects of the questionnaire.

The results show an internal discrepancy in the data between the percentage of individuals and couples reporting assets, and the percentage reporting income from rent, dividends and interest. (See Table 1.) Comparison with the 1959–60 survey shows that this mainly arose from a failure, in the national survey, to record very small amounts of interest income. These are the small sums of a few pounds a year which are often left to accumulate in a bank account. Such under-reporting is a common feature of surveys. Where such a discrepancy showed itself on an individual return in the 1959–60 survey, interest was imputed at a standard rate.[2] But as Table 1 shows there is also a higher percentage of the national sample reporting no assets at all than in the 1959–60 survey, when more research resources could be devoted to establishing the full asset picture. We may conclude that the national information is biassed downwards somewhat in respect of asset ownership and in respect of income from assets.

This alone would suggest that total recorded income in the survey was slightly lower than the true income of those people who did co-operate. Taken in conjunction with evidence that those people who did not co-operate fully tended to be rather better off, this would lead us to expect the survey income levels to be biassed downwards compared with the total population of the old. To test this we may compare the national survey data in a limited way with certain official estimates. Data from the Ministry of Pensions and National Insurance indicates that 84 per cent of individuals aged 65 and over are

---

1. For discussion of 'proxy' interviews, see Introduction, p. 13.
2. A similar procedure has been adopted by the U.S. Dept. of Health, Education and Welfare in their survey of the finances of the aged—see Epstein, L., "Income of the Aged in 1962. First Findings of the 1963 Survey of the Aged", *Social Security Bulletin*, March 1964. The difference between the percentage of units reporting rent, dividend and interest income in the 1959–60 Survey (using imputation) and the British cross-national Survey, see Table 1, p. 80 is if anything rather larger than the difference between the Department of Health, Education and Welfare survey and the American cross-national survey. The D.H.E.W. estimates are 63 per cent of the couples 45 per cent of the men and 50 per cent of the women reporting asset income. The American cross-national estimates are 42 per cent, 27 per cent and 35 per cent respectively.

TABLE 1

The percentage of income units with assets in the ranges stated and reporting income from rent, dividends and interest. A comparison between the 1962 and the 1959-60 surveys

Level of Assets	Men		Women		Couples	
	59/60	Britain 1962	59/60	Britain 1962	59/60	Britain 1962
None	26	35	37	41	22	30
Less than £100	19	15	18	18	18	16
£100 to £500	17	24	20	19	24	26
£500 or more	39	24	26	20	37	25
Unknown	—	2	—	2	—	2
Total	100	100	100	100	100	100
Percentage of all units reporting income from rent, dividends and interest	61	24	54	23	69	25

drawing a retirement pension.[1] Calculated as a percentage of individuals (not income units) the figure for our sample is 83 per cent. Again the official estimate of the percentage of retirement pensioner income units receiving supplementation from national assistance is 24 per cent, compared with an estimate of 26 per cent obtained from the present sample.

These differences are small; the differences between our data and certain Inland Revenue data are a little larger. In the course of their 1962–3 survey of personal incomes that Department prepared some special tabulations which related to the incomes of pensioners and aged persons, and which we were generously allowed to compare in aggregate with our national tabulations.[2] The Inland Revenue estimates exclude large numbers of elderly people whose incomes are below the tax exemption limit, and possibly also some of those whose incomes were below the special age exemption limit. In 1962–3 this age exemption limit meant that couples where one partner was aged 65 or over with an income above £480 a year, or single and widowed persons aged 65 or over with an income above £300 a year, were not liable to pay income tax. We cannot therefore, compare the two sets of data for the whole income distribution. Table 2 shows, first, the number of income units in the Inland Revenue tables with total incomes above £300 for single and widowed people and £450 for couples (the nearest intervals to the age exemption limit shown in the income distribution). Second, it shows an estimate of the number of income units with similar levels of income which has been obtained by applying the percentage of units above these income levels in the

1. *Report of the Ministry of Pensions and National Insurance*, 1964 Cmnd 2392, London, HMSO.
2. The published data for the 1962–3 survey of personal incomes is contained in the 107*th Report of the Commissioners of HM Inland Revenue*, Cmnd 2572, London, HMSO.

national survey income distributions to our estimate of the total number of elderly income units in the national population.

Estimated number of elderly income units with total incomes over £450 a year couples, and £300 a year single and widowed in 1962-63. A comparison between Inland Revenue and national survey (Britain 1962) estimates

	Couples with incomes over £450 a year	Single and widowed men with incomes over £300 a year	Single and widowed women with incomes over £300 a year
Inland Revenue estimates ...	850,333	218,863	632,592
National survey (Britain 1962) estimates	733,000	260,000	536,000

These comparisons are affected by the following factors:

(i) The Inland Revenue definition of total income is different from that adopted in the national survey.[1] In particular it includes schedule A income which is imputed income from owner-occupied houses. Inland Revenue income will therefore be higher than cross-national income.

(ii) The Inland Revenue tabulations for single and widowed women relate to women aged 60 and over. The cross-national data relate to income levels available to women 65 and over. But the figure in Table 2, column 3, has been obtained by applying the percentage of women 65 and over with incomes over £300 a year to the estimated total number of single and widowed women aged 60 and over. It is likely that women between the ages of 60–64 are rather better off than women 65 and over. If this is the case the national survey estimate of numbers will be biassed downwards for this reason and not because the national income totals are understated.

(iii) The national survey estimates have all been obtained on the assumption that the cases where total income was not known but where partial financial information was available were all incomes above the age exemption limit.

The national estimate of the number of couples and women with incomes in excess of the age exemption limit is 14 per cent and 16 per cent respectively below the corresponding Inland Revenue estimates; the national estimate for men is some 18 per cent higher than the Inland Revenue estimate. The exclusion of schedule A income from the national totals is probably the most important reason for expecting the national estimates to be lower although it cannot account for

1. For national survey definition see below p. 82. For Inland Revenue definition see Cmnd 2572, *op. cit.*, p. 80.

the whole of the differences. One thing which this comparison certainly justifies is the assumption that those cases which are shown in the 'no answer' category in the tables which follow all have incomes above the age exemption limit for tax purposes. Provided that assumption is made the comparison suggests that the national survey income distribution can be broadly relied upon. In the discussion that follows the 'no answer' cases will be treated on that assumption. Little, or no, reduction to allow for bias is then required in the percentages shown as falling in the lower income groups, upon which a lot of attention will be focussed in the following pages. As for figures of median incomes, the effect on these of assuming that the no answer cases all come in the upper income groups could be quite small and is certainly not likely to amount to more than ten shillings a week.[1] All of the bias dealt with in this discussion of reliability is, of course, additional to normal sampling error which is dealt with in Appendix 2. As surveys go it is not great and we have been able to put an order of magnitude upon it. The evidence that follows cannot, at any rate, be discounted by arguments (such as that 'people always understate income') which have been used on occasion to discount the results of surveys which cut across established pre-conceptions.

Some definitions

The financial part of he cross-national survey was concerned to establish a picture of the sources and levels of financial support available to older people in each of the three countries. The definitions adopted and the form of the analysis were dictated by the prime concern to make comparison between the three countries. One problem which had to be overcome was that of making inter-country comparisons with different units of currency. To facilitate comparison of a relative kind, we adopted the device, for many of the income tables, of expressing intervals of the income distribution as a percentage of the median income for each of the three types of income unit in each of the three countries. Unless this background is remembered the results for one country will look strange. It means that the income intervals used for discussing income distributions in some of the tables which follow are different for men, women and couples, and are of a different absolute size (see Table 3).

The priority given to cross-national comparisons also means that, with limited resources, we have not always, so far at any rate, been able to study as fully as we might have wished some aspects of the situation peculiar to Britain.

Total money income is defined to exclude capital gains or any other windfall receipts, and to include all regular sources of cash receipts such as regular allowances from children not members of the old person's household. Any help or income in kind is excluded and no attempt has been made to impute any rental for an owner-

---

1. See Table 5 below, p. 87.

TABLE 3

Income ranges used in the cross-national analysis (defined as a percentage of median total income for each type of income unit)

Income ranges for cross-national purposes	Equivalents in British currency £ per week (upper limit)		
	Men	*Women*	*Couples*
More than 20 per cent below median	Up to £3 12s.	Up to £2 19s.	Up to £5 19s.
More than 5 per cent up to 20 per cent below median ...	,, ,, £4 6s.	,, ,, £3 10s.	,, ,, £7 2s.
Up to 5 per cent below and above median total income	,, ,, £4 15s.	,, ,, £3 18s.	,, ,, £7 17s.
More than 5 per cent up to 20 per cent above median ...	,, ,, £5 9s.	,, ,, £4 8s.	,, ,, £9 0s.
More than 20 per cent up to 50 per cent above median ...	,, ,, £6 16s.	,, ,, £5 11s.	,, ,, £11 5s.
More than 50 per cent up to 100 per cent above median	,, ,, £9 2s.	,, ,, £7 8s.	,, ,, £15 0s.
More than 100 per cent above median	£9 3s. and over	£7 9s. and over	£15 1s. and over

occupied house. In treating a source of income as 'regular' we had to be guided by what the respondent said. Income is defined net of any business expenses, but gross before payment of taxes. The amount of income and the number of times it was received in the previous twelve months were recorded at the interview. When these receipts were not weekly they were converted to a weekly basis and the analysis is presented in terms of total gross weekly income.

Assets are defined to include cash, deposits in ordinary banks, the post office or trustee savings banks, building societies, etc., the holdings of stocks, shares, savings certificates, premium bonds, etc.' as well as the value of property in a business, land or buildings. The capital value of an annuity is ignored and the total income from the annuity treated as part of weekly income. The decision to exclude the surrender value of life and endowment policies and the value of owner-occupied houses from the definition of assets may require justification. It is difficult to establish the surrender value of insurance policies, and since only a minority of the sample reported sums insured of more than £100 it was clear that to try to establish this information would make little difference to the total asset picture. Many of these policies are kept as burial policies and scarcely cover the funeral expenses when the old person dies.

With owner-occupied houses the case for exclusion rests on the difficulty which an old person has in realising the whole or part of the capital which the house represents. Occasionally an old person would say that he or she would like to sell their house and get a smaller one, but "where" they asked "was such a house to be found?" The needs of older people have been slow to be recognised in the commercial housing field. As for raising a loan or a mortgage against the security of the house, this is not easy for most old people. Building societies give preference, particularly when their funds are short, to people who wish newly to acquire a house. Relatively few of the generation of old people with which we are concerned have experience of using banks, even if the banks were willing to make advances on this kind of security to this class of customer. Some people would disagree with our treatment however.[1] So while excluding the value of owner-occupied property and life assurance from our figure of total assets we nonetheless obtained such information as we could about these two assets.

Five main sources of income have been distinguished in the analysis, although sometimes information will be given relating to finer divisions than this. *State benefits* include retirement pensions, non-contributory old age pensions, national assistance, war or disability pensions. There were only six cases of unemployment or sickness benefit in the whole sample which are included in this category. *Employment income* includes both wages and salaries, casual earnings and income from business, farm or professional practice. *Employers' pensions* includes all regular payments financed in part, at least, by former employers and paid either directly by them, or through trusts or insurance companies to their employees or the widows of their employees. *Property income* is income from rent, dividends, interest and those annuities not arising from former employment. *Other income* is the remainder, including regular cash allowances from children, income from trade unions, friendly societies and charities; and income from lodgers and boarders net of expenses calculated on the basis of a standard scale which varied according to whether meals, heating, etc., were provided.

Throughout the period of the field-work the basic retirement pension for a single person was £2 17s. 6d. and for a man with a dependent wife was £4 12s. 6d. a week. National assistance scale rates—that is for requirements other than rent which is allowed for in addition—were increased between the two rounds of field work. At the time of the first round of interviews the scale rate for a single householder (someone directly responsible for rent and household necessaries) was £2 13s. 6d., for a single non-householder £2 9s. 6d., and for a couple £4 10s. 0d. a week. On 24th September 1962, before the start of the second stage of the survey in November, national assistance rates became £2 17s. 6d., £2 11s. 6d. and £4 15s. 6d. a week respectively. Comparison of the detailed income distributions of the first and second stages of the survey showed that this change in scale rates was scarcely detectable in the overall picture so the results from the two stages have been combined and the following data, unless otherwise indicated, relate to the full sample of 3,146 income units.

---

1. See for instance *Committee of Inquiry into the Impact of Rates on Households,* Cmnd 2582, HMSO, London, 1965, para. 293.

The composition of the financial sample

The sample of income units which we have is not identical with the sample of individuals described in Part I. As we have seen, women aged 65 or over married to men under 65 are excluded. Their husbands had not yet reached normal retirement age. For this reason alone our sample would not be representative of the total population over retirement age in this country. In addition, however, women aged between 60 and 65 (that is over the normal retirement age for women) were excluded unless they happened to be married to men who were 65 or over. In 1962 the total population over retirement age (60 for women and 65 for men) numbered nearly $7\frac{3}{4}$ millions; the population of men and women aged 65 and over numbered 6·1 millions. We estimate that our financial material describes the position of 6·5 million individuals contained within 4·9 million income units. Of these, 1·65 million were married couples where the husband was 65 or over, 708,000 were single or widowed men aged 65 or over and 2·5 million were single and widowed women aged 65 or over.

But how many of these income units were retirement pensioners and how many of them were still in full-time employment? Most, but not all, of the sample were retirement pensioners. Eight out of every 10 income units (a national total of 3·9 million units) were receiving a retirement pension.[1] These divide into two main groups, 2 out of every 10 of the sample receiving supplementation to their pension from the National Assistance Board, and the remainder, 6 out of 10 of the sample, without assistance. It should be noted that another small group, 5 per cent of the sample (national total: just under a quarter of a million units) were receiving national assistance without any retirement pension, although sometimes the assistance was supplementing other state income like a non-contributory old age pension, or a war or disability pension. A similar small group (another 5 per cent of the sample) were receiving one of these other forms of state benefit without national assistance. Altogether, 9 out of every 10 income units were receiving some sort of income from the state. Of the 1 in 10 without state benefits just over one half were in full-time employment. Most of these would ultimately be entitled to a retirement pension. The remainder of the group (national total: nearly a quarter of a million units) without state benefits were without entitlement to a pension, usually because they had not been insured under the pre-1948 scheme and were then too old to become insured under the National Insurance Act 1946. These people were living on pensions from former employers, or on property income. Ten cases in the whole sample revealed old people with no income at all, supported entirely by their families.

To what extent were these elderly people retired? They were all past retirement age, in the sense of being past the age at which the state retirement pension becomes payable if contribution and other conditions are satisfied. But retirement is a difficult concept to

---

1. All estimates of population totals are, of course, subject to sampling error. See Appendix 2.

85

define. Some had part-time employment; a few did occasional jobs. If, however, retirement is defined as giving up full-time employment then 9 out of every 10 income units were retired. Of the 1 in 10 in full-time employment as we saw above, about half were postponing drawing their retirement pension; the other half were combining a retirement pension and full-time earnings.[1]

The description of income levels which follows refers to the position in 1962. But in addition to the increase in national assistance scale rates which took place during the course of the field-work, both retirement pensions and scale rates have been increased twice between then and March 1965. The changes are summarised in Table 4.

TABLE 4

Changes in the levels of the retirement pension and national assistance scale rates between April 1961 and March 1965

	Retirement Pension £ per week		National Assistance scale rate £ per week		
	Couple	Single person	Couple	Single House-holder	Single non-House-holder
	£ s. d.	£ s. d.	£ s. d.	£ s. d.	£ s. d.
April 1961	4 12 6	2 17 6	4 10 0	2 13 6	2 9 6
Sept. 1962	—	—	4 15 6	2 17 6	2 11 6
May 1963	5 9 0	3 7 6	5 4 6	3 3 6	2 15 0
March 1965	6 10 0	4 0 0	6 5 6	3 16 0	3 7 6

Absolute levels of income available to the elderly have, therefore, increased over the past three years. So too have prices and the extent to which these changes represent a real increase, and the extent to which any conclusions drawn from the survey data should be modified in the light of this, will be discussed in Chapter 7.

The level of total weekly income

One of the first features to be noted in Table 5 about the income levels of the sample is how close large numbers were to the then prevailing levels of the retirement pension. This may be somewhat surprising because it is widely held that most old people have some other source of income with which to supplement their pension. If national assistance is included as a source this is true; but the amounts received from private sources like employers pensions are as we shall see, often small and no more than a few shillings a week. Table 5 shows that 23 per cent of the women and 13 per cent

---

1. This can be done, without any reduction of the pension, by men when they reach the age of 70 and women when they reach the age of 65. We are here discussing income units, however, and it is possible that in addition to combining a reduced pension with full-time earnings one partner in a couple could be drawing a retirement pension and the other be in full-time employment.

TABLE 5

Percentage of elderly income units with total gross weekly money income in the ranges stated; Britain 1962

Range of total gross weekly income £ per week	Men		Women		Couples	
	Per cent of sample	Estimated number of units in population	Per cent of sample	Estimated number of units in population	Per cent of sample	Estimated number of units in population
Up to £3	13	92,000	23	575,000	8 }	132,000
£3 up to £3 10s.	11	78,000	16	400,000		
£3 10s. up to £4	12	85,000	17	425,000		
£4 up to £4 10s.	9 }	106,000	10	250,000		
£4 10s. up to £5	6 }		8	200,000		
£5 up to £6	12	85,000	8	200,000	16	264,000
£6 up to £7	7 }	78,000	4	100,000	18	297,000
£7 up to £8	4 }		2 }		10	165,000
£8 up to £10	7	49,000	2 }	100,000	14	231,000
£10 up to £15	6 }	78,000	1 }		17	279,000
£15 up to £20	3 }			100,000	6	99,000
£20 and over	2				5	83,000
No income	2 cases		6 cases	—	2 cases	—
No answer[1]	8	56,000	6	150,000	6	99,000
Total percentage	100	—	100	—	100	—
Number of cases[2]	495	707,000	1,552	2,500,000	1,099	1,650,000
Median income of known cases	£4 11s.	—	£3 14s.	—	£7 10s.	—

Note: Estimated population numbers are subject to sampling error. See Appendix 2.

1. These 'no answer' cases are assumed all to fall above £6 a week for men and women and £9 a week for couples. See above p 82.
2. The population estimates are rounded. For method of estimation see Appendix 3.

87

of the men had incomes of less than £3 a week. More than half of the women and 36 per cent of the men had weekly incomes below £4 a week. The couples were better off, but even there 8 per cent had incomes of less than £5 a week and another 16 per cent had incomes between £5 and £6 a week; that is altogether nearly a quarter with weekly incomes below £6 a week.

Translating these sample estimates into population totals would suggest that nearly 1½ million women and a quarter of a million men had total weekly incomes of less than £4; and some 400,000 couples had total weekly incomes below £6. The median income of the women was only 16s. 6d. a week, that of the men 34s. 6d., and that of the couples 57s. 6d., above the then prevailing levels of the retirement pension.[1]

It is difficult to compare these medians with what may be called the contemporary definition of subsistence, which is the national assistance scale rate. Variable rents complicate the picture and we shall discuss the effect of this below.[2] But in 1962 the average rent allowance paid to retirement pensioners receiving help from the National Assistance Board was 22s. 1d. a week.[3] The total of the rent allowance and the scale rates might then be said to represent the 'average' needs of an old person. Rounded to the nearest shilling a week the figure was £3 15s. for a single householder and £5 12s. for a couple.

The median income of the women in our sample was £3 14s. a week, so that very nearly half of all single and widowed women had incomes below this subsistence total. A quarter of the single and widowed men were below it, and another quarter no more than a fifth above it. Thirteen per cent of the couples had incomes below this subsistence total and approximately another 18 per cent had incomes no more than a fifth above it.

Comparisons with the rest of the population

If one aspect of contemporary poverty is relative or comparative deprivation, it is important to ask: How do these levels of income compare with the levels enjoyed by other sections of the community? The difficulty is that no single comparison is meaningful for all purposes. One of the most striking of such comparisons is with personal disposable per capita income. This is a money measure of the resources available to private individuals after payment of taxes, which gives children equivalent shares with adults. In 1962 the figure was £7 6s. per week for the population as a whole. The median incomes in Table 5 look low by comparison, even that of the couples

---

1. The medians quoted are always the medians of the known cases. If, as we have said, it is reasonable to assume that the 'no answer' cases belong to the upper end of the income distribution, the median might be raised by a few shillings. See above p. 82.

2. See p. 112 onwards.

3. *Report of the National Assistance Board*, Cmnd 2078, London, HMSO, p. 21.

being £3 5s. a week on a per capita basis. Frequently comparison is made with levels of average earnings. This practice has been stimulated by current interest in schemes for the wage-relation of social security benefits in general, and of retirement pensions in particular. In October 1962 average adult male earnings for manual workers covered by the Ministry of Labour's six-monthly inquiry were £15 17s. per week.[1] A rough approximation to the median can be obtained from the Ministry of Labour's figures of earnings distribution in 1960, and allowing for the increase in earnings between 1960 and 1962, it suggests a level of median earnings for adult male manual workers of a little over £15 a week. That figure is twice the median income of the couples in our sample, and more than four times the median income of the women. It can be objected that the 'average' wage earner has to support a young family, and however difficult it may be to delineate differences of 'need' in other areas, this is one where clearly the 'needs' of an old person are less. The great majority of people over 65 have no dependants to support (other than a wife).

Another comparison of some interest might be between the income levels available generally, irrespective of age, to couples without dependants, and to single and widowed men and to single and widowed women, also without dependants. Such a comparison is possible with the use of Inland Revenue data from the survey of personal incomes in 1962–3. That survey provides an income distribution for income units classified by number of dependants and family size, which enables couples and single and widowed persons without dependants to be studied alone.[2] These data exclude all units with incomes below £180 a year (the tax exemption limit) and also exclude some married couples with incomes above £180 a year where those incomes are derived entirely from national insurance benefits. It appears from the unpublished tabulations referred to earlier that nearly 60 per cent of elderly income units are excluded.[3] In this sense the data approximate to distributions of income for married couples and single people with no dependants excluding, to a very large extent, the people over 65 with whom the present comparison is to be made.

Median incomes were first obtained by interpolation from the published tax data. They are no more than orders of magnitude. But then some allowance had to be made for the fact that the majority of elderly people will not be liable for income tax. Certainly anyone with the median income or below, of the units in our sample would not have been paying tax in 1962. On the other hand the ordinary population had median incomes at levels which were taxable. An extremely rough calculation of tax liability at the median income level in the ordinary population was made and the figures shown in Table 6

---

1   The industries covered are manufacturing industries generally, mining and quarrying (except coal), construction, gas, electricity and water, transport and communication.

2.   Cmnd 2572, *op. cit.*, Tables 78–81.

3.   See above, p. 80.

may then be described as the net income after tax available to recipients of the median gross income for the various types of tax unit shown there.

In every case the Inland Revenue income levels are well above those available to the elderly, ranging from roughly two-thirds above in the case of couples where the wives are not working, to twice as high in the case of the men and women, and to two and a half times in the case of couples where wives were earning. The position of the men and women is particularly striking since in the Inland Revenue

TABLE 6

Median gross incomes net of income tax in 1962-3 for certain types of income unit, compared with the median incomes of the sample of elderly income units; Britain 1962

Type of income unit	Median income net of tax from Inland Revenue data[1]	Median income from the national survey (Britain 1962)
	£ per week	£ per week
Married couple tax units with no dependants		
(i) wives earning	£19	£7 10s.
(ii) wives not earning	£13	
Single male and widower tax units with no dependants	£10	£4 11s.
Single female and widow tax units with no dependants	£7	£3 14s.

data these groups will contain a high proportion of boys and girls who have only been working for a few years and who would tend to depress the level of the median.

In Table 3 we showed the income intervals used for the analysis of our survey data, defined as a percentage of the median income for each type of income unit. It is interesting to find that what are the 'high' or very top income groups used for classifying the incomes of the aged are at, or even below, the levels of the median incomes of the tax units in the Inland Revenue data. In other words the 'high' incomes of the old are the 'middling' incomes for their younger counterparts.

The effect of asset ownership

Would this picture be changed much if it is extended to take account of asset ownership? We know generally that the proportion of people with assets and the average value of such assets, tends to

---

1. All figures here are rounded to the nearest pound.

increase as people get older up to about the age of retirement, then to decline again, but not to levels as low as those encountered say below the age of 30 or 35.[1]   If we could take all financial resources into account, then, the comparison we have just made between the old and other age groups might be shifted in favour of the aged; however, an examination of Table 7 which analyses the asset position of our sample in relation to income level suggests that the shift would not be very great.

Well over a third of all income units (35 per cent of the men, 41 per cent of women and 30 per cent of couples) had no assets at all, and another 15 to 18 per cent had less than £100.   Between a fifth and a quarter of all units reported total assets worth more than £500, but, as is to be expected, the ownership of these assets is correlated with income. (See Table 7.)   In the lowest of the median income groups (that is up to £3 10s. or £3 12s. for men and women and £7 2s. for couples) between 40 and 50 per cent of the units had no assets at all.   On the other hand between 10 and 20 per cent in those income groups had assets of more than £500.

Interest received on assets is already included in total income. But should an assessment of the financial resources of the aged assume that capital will be consumed to support living standards, and, if so, at what rate?   It has been suggested that the most satisfactory way would be to assume that each individual will consume his or her assets evenly over the number of years of their remaining life expectancy, and, in the analysis, to increase income levels by the appropriate share of assets.[2]   This is a very stringent assumption because in the real world few individuals will know how long they have to live.   In any case our survey does not provide the data necessary to do this. In Table 8 (page 94), however, the information on income and assets is brought in a way which will enable the reader to exercise his own judgment about the weight to be accorded to the ownership of assets.

In the whole sample 40 per cent of the single people and couples had incomes more than 5 per cent below the median income of their particular type of income unit.   These people could, as we have seen, be said to have low incomes.   But it might be argued that where they had assets of £100 or more they could supplement their income for a year or two.   Table 8 shows that 14 per cent of them were in that position.   On the most stringent criteria—that is income more than 5 per cent below the median, and no assets or assets of less than £100, we find 26 per cent of the sample (or the equivalent of 1¼ million income units in the population) had what must be described as

---

1.   Lydall, H., "The Life Cycle in Income, Saving and Asset Ownership", *Econometrica* Vol. 23, No. 2, 1955.   Revell, J. R. S., "Assets and Age", *Bulletin of the Oxford Institute of Statistics* Vol. 24, No. 3, 1962.   But some of the improvement shown in these data is due to older people more often owning their own houses mortgage free.   We have argued the case for excluding the value of owner-occupied houses in estimates of assets in studies of the present kind.   See above p. 83.

2.   Epstein, L., 1964, *op. cit.*

TABLE 7

Percentage of elderly income units in median income groups owning assets in the ranges stated; Britain 1962

	Men					
	Range of total assets					Total Percentage (Number of cases)
Range of total weekly income £ per week	No Assets	less than £100	£100 up to £500	£500 or more	No answer	
Up to £3 12s.	45	14	25	15	2	100 (143)
,, ,, £4 6s.	37	32	11	17	2	100 (65)
,, ,, £4 15s.	48	7	24	21	—	100 (29)
,, ,, £5 9s.	43	12	18	23	4	100 (51)
,, ,, £6 16s.	37	13	32	18	—	100 (56)
£6 17s. and over	22	12	28	37	2	100 (110)
No answer	12	17	22	49	—	100 (41)
All income groups	35	15	24	24	2	100 (495)

Table 7—continued

Women

		43	19	24	11	3	100 (350)
Up to £2 19s.	...	43	19	24	11	3	100 (350)
,, ,, £3 10s.	...	50	23	16	10	1	100 (278)
,, ,, £3 18s.	...	53	16	17	12	2	100 (207)
,, ,, £4 8s.	...	46	24	16	13	1	100 (188)
,, ,, £5 11s.	...	43	21	18	17	—	100 (203)
£5 12s. and over	...	21	11	22	45	1	100 (228)
No answer	...	15	6	19	55	4	100 (98)
All income groups	...	41	18	19	20	2	100 (1,552)

Couples

Up to £5 9s.	...	38	17	24	18	3	100 (256)
,, ,, £7 2s.	...	44	19	22	14	1	100 (216)
,, ,, £7 17s.	...	34	23	27	16	—	100 (82)
,, ,, £9 0s.	...	31	21	34	12	2	100 (99)
,, ,, £11 2s.	...	24	10	31	33	2	100 (137)
£11 6s. and over	...	14	13	23	47	2	100 (231)
No answer	...	10	14	30	31	15	100 (78)
All income groups	...	30	16	26	25	3	100 (1,099)

extremely low *total* financial resources. A modest relaxation either of the asset criterion to include people with assets between £100 and £500, or of the income criterion to include people with incomes no more than 5 per cent above the median but still with assets of less than £100 would take in one third of all the sample (or the equivalent of 1·6 million income units). This is one estimate of the size of the group which might be described as 'poor', using those quite arbitrary levels of income and assets which we have decided to call 'very low'. The use of different criteria, such as matching resources against estimated need in the same way as the National Assistance Board do, will as we shall see, yield a larger estimate of the numbers close to contemporary subsistence standards.[1]

TABLE 8

The percentage of all elderly income units with incomes and assets in the ranges stated; Britain 1962

Range of total gross weekly income	Percentage of the total number of income units with assets of:				All units
	None or less than £100	£100 up to £500	£500 or more	No answer	
More than 20 per cent below median	14	6	3		24
More than 5 per cent up to 20 per cent below median ...	12	3	2		18
Up to 5 per cent above and below median	7	2	1		10
More than 5 per cent up to 20 per cent above median	7	2	2	2	11
More than 20 per cent up to 50 per cent above median ...	7	3	3		12
More than 50 per cent up to 100 per cent above median ...	3	3	3		9
More than 100 per cent above median	2	2	5		9
No answer	2	2	3		7
Sum of four columns = 100 per cent					100
Number of cases					3,146

Owner-occupation and life insurance

The reasons for excluding the value of owner-occupied houses and of insurance from our definition of assets have been explained.[2] Information about these assets was collected, however, and is presented here so that any reader may make some allowance for them if he wishes. Thirty-one per cent of all people (27 per cent of the men,

---

1. See below p. 119.
2. See above p. 83–84.

94

27 per cent of the women and 38 per cent of the couples) were home owners. They were asked to place a current market valuation upon their house. Their replies must be treated with caution because few are likely to have had any recent experience of the market. Indeed a fifth said that they could not give a figure. But of those that gave a reply 16 per cent valued their house at less than £1,000, 25 per cent valued it between £1,000 up to £2,000, another 25 per cent between £2,000 up to £3,000 and the remainder at more than £3,000.

As for life and endowment insurance, 59 per cent of the sample said they had such insurance. Again it was more common for the couples than for the men and the women. But the amounts were small. Of those with insurance, 56 per cent had sums insured of less than £50, a third sums between £50 and £100 and only 11 per cent sums of more than £100. Again the amounts should be viewed with caution because it is doubtful how accurately these old people will know what their policies are worth. But these figures confirm the general impression that most of the insurance of this age group is what is termed 'burial insurance', and that the inclusion of the surrender value of such policies would make very little difference to the total asset picture.

Summary

Much of this chapter has been taken up with a general discussion of the definitions to be used in the analysis of financial resources and with an assessment of some of the limitations of the survey estimates. The conclusion is that the income and asset figures as revealed by the survey data may be slightly understated; but our discussion has shown that due allowance can be made for this. From our figures, on the most conservative basis, it still appears that in 1962, 1¾ million men and women aged 65 or over had total incomes of less than £4 a week, and 400,000 couples had total incomes of less than £6 a week. The picture can be improved a little by taking account of assets; but still 26 per cent of the sample (or 1¼ million income units) had minimal assets combined with very low incomes. Whatever standards we care to take in making a comparison between the income of the elderly and the population generally, whether it be personal disposable per capita income, average earnings, or some other measure, we are left with this result: *the aged have income levels a half or more below the levels of the population generally.*

CHAPTER 5

Characteristics of Old People with the Smallest Incomes

The importance of the state

In view of what we have already seen of the levels of total income available to the old people in our sample, and what we know about the levels of the retirement pension and national assistance, it is clear that a substantial number of the aged must derive all, or most, of their income from state sources. In fact 7 out of 10 people in the sample received their single largest source of income from the state. Other income sources like property income, employer's pension, or even earnings were the largest source of income for only a very small percentage (less than 10 per cent in every case). No less than 37 per cent of all the income units in the sample received all of their income from the state and another 15 per cent had less than £1 a week of non-state income.

TABLE 9

Percentage of elderly income units dependent upon state benefits; Britain 1962[1]

Dependence upon state benefits	Men	Women	Couples	All units
Nothing but state benefits (solely dependent)	34	49	20	37
Up to £1 a week non-state income (primarily dependant)...	15	18	12	15
Other (including no answer) ...	51	33	68	48
Total percentage	100	100	100	100
Number of cases	(197)	(607)	(430)	(1,233)

On the evidence presented in Table 9 it would not be unreasonable to conclude that a half of all old people were dependent solely or primarily upon the state for their income. In terms of population estimates they would number 2·45 million income units.

A more detailed distribution of non-state income is given in Table 10 and one of the interesting points to emerge is that while a half of elderly people depend upon the state, a quarter have more than £4 a week of non-state income. If it is assumed that a high proportion of the 'No answers' are also elderly people with relatively large amounts of non-state income, between a quarter and a third have more than £4 a week of non-state income.

1. Data from stage II of sample only (see above p. 12).

TABLE 10

Percentage of elderly income units with amounts of non-state income in the ranges stated[1]; Britain 1962

Range of non-state income shillings per week	Men	Women	Couples	All income Units
Nothing but State income ...	34	50	19	37
Non-state income:				
up to 5s.	3	5	3	4
,, ,, 10s.	6	5	3	4
,, ,, 15s.	3	3	3	3
,, ,, 20s.	4	5	4	4
,, ,, 30s.	4	3	7	5
,, ,, 40s.	7	2	4	3
,, ,, 60s.	9	5	7	7
,, ,, 80s.	4	4	7	5
,, ,, 100s.	2	2	5	3
101s and over	14	8	28	16
No answer	10	8	9	9
Total percentage	100	100	100	100

Non-state sources of income

Between a fifth and a quarter of all the people in the sample were receiving employment income, an employer's pension or some income from rent, dividends or interest.

TABLE 11

Percentage of elderly income units with income from different sources; Britain 1962

Percentage of units having income from:	Men	Women	Couples	All units
Earnings	21	10	34	20
Employer's Pension	36	11	43	26
Rent, interest and dividends ...	24	23	25	24
Other income combined ...	9	14	11	12
(i) Lodgers	2	7	5	6
(ii) Help from relatives ...	2 cases	3	1	2
(iii) Trade Union, charities, etc.	5	2	5	3

The relative importance of these sources of income, as measured by frequency of receipt, varied, particularly between the men and couples on the one hand, and women on the other. But the relative importance of these sources of income also varied in terms of the amounts received. An indication of these amounts is given in Table 12, where the median receipt from each source is shown, together with, for comparison, the median receipt from state benefits. Income from

---

1 People with no income from the state will be shown in the income interval appropriate to their total income.

earnings stands out as being by far the most important source of income in terms of income level.

TABLE 12

Median weekly income from different sources for those elderly income units receiving such income;[1] Britain 1962

Source of income	Men	Women	Couples
State benefits combined	£3 1s. (431)	£2 19s. (1,459)	£4 19s. (970)
Full time employment[2]	£9 12s. (50)	£5 0s. (45)	£10 10s. (186)
Part-time employment[2]	£3 0s. (33)	£1 5s. (92)	£3 2s. (95)
Employer's Pension	£1 17s. (168)	£1 18s. (155)	£2 4s. (436)
Rent, dividends and interest ...	15s. (97)	18s. (296)	15s. (242)
All other income	12s. (39)	£1 0s. (206)	16s. (120)

(i) *Earnings* Only 10 per cent of the women, but 21 per cent of the men and 34 per cent of the couples had employment income from either full or part-time activity.[3] Moreover, only 3 per cent of the women were working full-time compared with 18 per cent of the husbands in couples and 11 per cent of the men. The picture of earnings' levels of the couples is affected by the fact that wives' earnings (9 per cent of them were employed) have been amalgamated with those of their husbands. But not only did women less often receive employment income, the amount they received was less than half that of the couples. Nevertheless there is likely to be a considerable gap between the total income of any old person, man, women or couple still in employment, and their counterpart who had retired. This is well illustrated in Table 13. There the couples only are shown because the numbers of men and women are rather few, although the contrast between the retired and the employed is the same for them.

Over a half of the retired couples had incomes below £7 a week and 30 per cent had less than £6 a week; but only 4 per cent of those still working full-time were in the lowest income group with less than £7 a week. At the other end of the income scale, only a quarter of the retired (including all the no answer cases) had more than £10 a week income compared with 78 per cent of those still working full-time.

Another way of illustrating the importance of employment income in raising the income levels of the old, is to examine how far those in

1. The numbers in brackets are the number of known cases from which the medians have been calculated.
2. Wives' and husbands' earnings are combined and the classification of full or part-time depends upon the employment status of the husband.
3. The number of cases of self-employment income or income from farm, business or profession was so small that it was not distinguished in the analysis.

TABLE 13

Distribution of total income of elderly couples according to the employment status of the husband; Britain 1962

Range of total weekly income grouped £ per week	Husband in full-time employment	Husband in part-time employment	Husband retired
£5 up to £6	3	7	30
£6 up to £7	1	13	23
£7 up to £8	4	11	11
£8 up to £10	12	34	12
£10 up to £15	34	24	12
£15 up to £20	24	6	2
£20 and over	13	2	3
No answer	7	4	7
Total percentage	100	100	100
Number of cases	(204)	(101)	(770)

the top income groups of the total distribution were there largely by virtue of their employment income. Whereas only 18 per cent of all the couples were in full-time employment, 50 per cent of those in the highest income group (that is over £15 a week) were in full-time employment, and 14 per cent were there by virtue of employment income alone. The same is true of the men and to a lesser extent of the women. In the income groups over £10 a week a fifth of the women were in full-time employment (compared with 3 per cent overall). But none were there by virtue of employment income alone. In contrast, however, 11 per cent of the women were in the top income group by virtue of property income alone.

It would not be an exaggeration to say that there are two classes among the over-65s with significantly different income experience— those who can and do continue to work and those who can't or don't. The division is not very important for women, who nearly all fall into the second class, but it is important for men and couples. Often, in discussing the financial position of the elderly it is the retired who are primarily of interest. What then happens to the level of median income if those with employment income are excluded? As was to be expected the median level of the women's incomes was virtually unaffected (being in fact reduced by one shilling a week to £3 13s.). But the median income of the retired men was £4 3s. compared with £4 11s. for all men over 65; and of the retired couples it was only £6 13s. compared with £7 10s. for all couples over 65.

The amount of income old people received from employment was, on average, high compared with the amounts which they received from other non-state sources. People who were earning were markedly better off than those who weren't. But this was partly due to the fact that they combined employment income with other sources of income. To take the couples as an example once more, we found only 5 per cent of them with earnings as a single source of income. But

12 per cent had earnings combined with state benefits, and 10 per cent had earnings, state benefits plus another source of income.

The data available in fact suggest that elderly men's earnings were low compared with the average level of male earnings in the population as a whole. At the time of our field-work, the median of adult male manual workers' earnings was a little over £15 a week. The median income from employment of the couples in our sample, where the husband was working full-time was only £10 10s. (which will include some wives' earnings) and of the men £9 12s. Those in our sample who retired in the three years before they were interviewed were asked what their earnings had been before they retired. Their answers have to be treated with caution, but confirm the general impression that older men receive below average earnings.

Part of this phenomenon may be attributed to the occupational structure (more of the older men were probably working in declining industries where earnings are likely to be lower) which would not necessarily represent a decline in income for the individual. Part may be due to the tendency for manual workers, at any rate, to reach their peak earning strength in their late thirties and early forties.[1] Part may also be due to a tendency where ill-health occurs, in later working life, to move into less skilled and more menial but light occupations. More will be known about this process when the occupational data from the survey are analysed.

Further study of these various influences is badly needed, and in particular a study of what happens to the individual's standard of living in real terms where he or she retires. Even if there is a gradual decline in real earnings in the years approaching retirement, which culminates in a sharp drop on retirement, what this means in terms of living standards depends also upon what is happening to the number of dependents the man has to support, and to the position of other earners (particularly the wife).[2] The fact is that the actual drop in income on retirement cannot be measured by any over-simple comparison between, say, the level of the retirement pension and the level of average earnings of the working population, although this is not to say that average earnings do not provide a useful yardstick against which to measure the general pension level.

(ii) *Employers' pensions* were the income source, after state benefits, most frequently received by older people. The overall percentage with such income however, masks a considerable gulf between the men and the couples, of whom 36–43 per cent were receiving such pensions, and the women, of whom only 11 per cent were receiving them (see Table 11). Just under a half of these pensions were in respect of employment with the central and local government, in one capacity or another. The amounts of pension were very small. Nearly a quarter of the income units were receiving less than £1 a

---

1. Lydall, H., 1955, *op. cit.*
2. See Cole, Dorothy and Utting, J., "The Distribution of Household and Individual Income", *Income and Wealth Series VI*, Bowes and Bowes, London, 1956, for a discussion of changes in life cycle income related to changes in family size.

week, and just under another quarter between £1 and £2 a week. The upper levels could be high in individual cases, but less than a fifth of all units with employers' pensions were receiving more than £5 a week from them. These figures suggest that for the great majority of the old today employers' pensions are still non-existent or at the most are small supplements to the state retirement pension, rather than in any sense a substitute for such a pension.

In view of the rapid increase in recent years of the coverage of private pension schemes, the older age groups in the sample might be expected to be at a disadvantage in respect of this type of income. There is some suggestion in the material that employers' pensions are less available higher up the age range. Between the age groups 65–69 and 75 and over, the percentage of units receiving such pensions falls from 45 per cent to 38 per cent for couples, 39 per cent to 34 per cent for men and 16 per cent to 7 per cent for women. The level of the median receipt from these pensions also falls with age for couples, but not for men and women. Since employers' pensions have been much more common for certain classes of work and in certain occupational groups, these figures could well be affected by differential mortality rates among different occupational groups. But using a broad definition of social class we find that the trend with age is similar for both 'white collar' and 'blue collar' workers.[1]

TABLE 14

Percentage of retired elderly men (single, widowed and married) in different social classes and age groups who were receiving employers' pensions;[2] Britain 1962

Percentage of social class group with pension	Age group			All
	65–69	70–74	75+	
Blue collar	56	38	37	43
(Number of cases)	(113)	(78)	(97)	(288)
White collar	73	59	45	59
(Number of cases)	(73)	(49)	(42)	(164)

Table 14 relates only to those men who have completely retired and also excludes service workers; so that the percentages with employers' pensions differ from those for the whole sample of men. In the age group 65–69, 56 per cent of the retired blue collar men had employers' pensions but only 37 per cent in the age group of 75 and over. As many as 73 per cent of the retired white collar men had pensions in the age group 65–69 but only 45 per cent in the age group of 75 and over. If these figures can be taken as a guide, it appears that both blue collar and white collar occupational pensions have been

---

1. The social class definition is for cross-national purposes and is that used by the U.S. Department of Commerce. It derives from a classification of 'main' occupation during working life.
2. Men here includes husbands in couples.

increasing over recent years but the gap between the social classes in the extent of coverage remains.

The coverage of employers' pensions for women is interesting. Even among single women who are likely to have more consistent work records than widows, only 18 per cent were receiving an employer's pension. The corresponding figure for widows was 9 per cent. Some of the widows in our sample will have lost their husband before he, the husband, had reached retiring age and begun to draw any employer's pension to which he might have been entitled. Nevertheless these figures must mean that the bulk of employers' pensions die with the recipient, even though in some cases, the widow may receive a lump sum at her husband's death. In the 1959/60 survey 10 per cent of the widows reported that their husband's pension had ceased when he died. There is little support to be found in this data for the view that private superannuation arrangements are taking over from the state. The majority of old people, women included, even in the age group 65–69 are without such pensions and for another substantial proportion they are at levels which make them little more than useful additions to other sources of income.

(iii) *Rent, dividends and interest* were being received by about a quarter of all income units, men, women and couples (see Table 11). The reasons for believing that these figures underestimate the true percentage with such income and also the reasons for believing that the ommissions were mostly of small amounts, have been discussed earlier (page 79). The amounts actually reported as being received were also low. The median income from this source, of those reporting property income, was less than £1 a week (see Table 12) and another 15 per cent reported amounts between £1 and £2 a week. Only 15 per cent of all the units in the sample reported receiving more than £5 a week. Both in terms of frequency and level of receipt then, property income is a less important source than employers' pensions for the aged. Women are the exception to this. Property income was one of the sources where they were relatively well placed as compared with couples and men, both in terms of the proportions receiving it and of the amounts being received.

(iv) *Other income* was a mixed bag, as can be seen from Table 11 where the most important components—income from lodgers and boarders, income from trade unions or charitable grants, and regular cash help from relatives—are shown separately. The percentage of units receiving such income ranged from only 14 per cent of the women to 9 per cent of the men and the amounts were very small indeed. Again, as with property, more than a half reported receipts of less than £1 a week; another quarter reported receipts of between £1 and £2; and only 5 per cent were receiving more than £5 a week.

The regular cash help from relatives included here does not, of course, exhaust the help which children and others extend to their aged relatives. Much of this help is in kind—gifts of food, clothing and help with holidays, outings and so on. Through very general questions this survey has confirmed that such help is extensive. In

102

the 1959/60 survey detailed questions were asked to enable a money value to be placed upon such help where the old people were living on their own.[1] The task of valuing help where old and young people are sharing house is more difficult as we shall see below.[2] But the 1959/60 survey showed that between 60 per cent of the women and a third of the couples living alone were receiving help, and that in most cases it was worth upwards of two or three shillings a week. At the same time the study revealed the importance of the two-way transaction involved in 'help'. Grandparents and others wish to reciprocate where they can. In discussing standards of living achieved by the old this extensive network of family exchange must certainly be remembered. At the same time in discussing the 'needs' of old people, the need to be independent, and to be able to play a part as giver as well as receiver, must also be borne in mind.

Combination of sources of income

To receive some non-state income in addition to state benefits could mean having little more than a few shillings a week on top of the retirement pension. In Table 10 we saw that 52 per cent of the sample had no income or less than £1 a week from non-state sources. Another 8 per cent had between £1 and £2. In many of these cases the six shillings from the railway pension, or the fifteen shillings from a few hours cleaning were substitutes or alternatives to applying for national assistance, rather than serving to raise these old people's income levels far above the assistance level.

But if the old person was fortunate enough to combine two or more such sources of income with a retirement pension, then a substantial difference could be made to the level of total income received.[3] Combining income sources in this way was not uncommon. Forty-two per cent of all men, women and couples had only one source of income; 41 per cent had two sources, and 17 per cent had three or more. More than 40 per cent of each type of unit in the two top income groups combined two sources of income, and in the highest income group, 27 per cent of the men, 43 per cent of the women and 47 per cent of the couples, had three or more sources of income. There was, in fact, a close correlation between numbers of sources of income and total income level.

In drawing together this discussion of the income sources of the elderly it should be noted that the state remains the most important financial provider in old age. To say that a half of all elderly people are primarily dependent upon the state is not inconsistent with saying that many old people also have income from other sources. The amounts of income from such sources vary enormously from a few shillings to several pounds a week, but mostly they are small. The

---

1. See Cole, Dorothy with Utting, J., *op. cit.*, 1962, Chapter VII.
2. See p. 111 onwards.
3. Source of income is here defined as one of the five main sources described on p. 84 above.

better off among the old are those who are still working or who combine together two or three income sources (of which, of course, one may be employment income). The close association between the receipt of particular sources of income, or of several sources of income and income level is best summarised in Table 15, which shows the percentage of units in each quartile of the income distribution receiving income from each of the sources just discussed. At the lowest income levels, for all types of income unit, state benefits predominate. As we move up the income scale so the other sources of income become more important.

TABLE 15

Percentage of all elderly units in each income quartile receiving income from each source;[1] Britain 1962

(Percentage with income from each source)

	Income Quartile			
	Highest	2nd highest	2nd lowest	Lowest
Men (range of income)	£6 13s. and over	£4 11s. up to £6 13s.	£3 8s. up to £4 11s.	Up to £3 8s.
Earnings	46·9	17·7	6·1	2·6
State benefits	63·7	94·7	100·0	95·6
Employer's pension ...	46·9	51·3	33·3	10·5
Property	30·1	27·4	15·8	12·3
Other	12·4	12·4	6·1	2·6
Number of cases	113	113	114	114
Women (range of income) ...	£4 14s. and over	£3 14s. up to £4 14s.	£3 up to £3 14s.	Up to £3
Earnings	24·8	8 8	3·8	0·5
State benefits	87·3	97·0	98·9	95·9
Employer's pension ...	23·1	10·7	5·7	1·4
Property	40·5	16·8	14·3	9·1
Other	25·9	18·7	6·3	3·3
Number of cases	363	363	364	364
Couples (range of income) ...	£10 18s. and over	£7 10s. up to £10 18s.	£6 up to £7 10s.	Up to £6
Earnings	67·8	45·5	14·1	5·5
State benefits	71·0	87·5	98·8	97·7
Employer's pension ...	47·8	52·5	47·5	19·9
Property	35·7	27·1	16·9	13·7
Other	10·2	11·4	13·7	8·2
Number of cases	255	255	255	256

1. The income quartile is the range of the income distribution which includes exactly one quarter of all cases.

Age and income

The evidence that income level declines as age increases is strong. There was more than £2 a week difference in our sample between the median income of the couples and men aged 75 and over and those aged 65–69, and still a difference, although a much smaller one of nine shillings a week, for the women.

TABLE 16

Median total weekly income by age group for all elderly income units and those who are retired; Britain 1962

(£ per week)

| Type of income unit | Age group | | | | | | | |
| | 65–69 | | 70–74 | | 75+ | | All age groups | |
	All units	Ret'd only	All units	Ret'd only	All units	Ret'd only	All units	Ret'd only
Men ...	£6 7s.	£4 12s.	£4 11s.	£4 3s.	£4 2s.	£4 0s.	£4 11s.	£4 2s.
Women ...	£4 0s.	£3 15s.	£3 14s.	£3 12s.	£3 11s.	£3 10s.	£3 14s.	£3 13s.
Couples ...	£8 16s.	£7 2s.	£7 7s.	£6 15s.	£6 9s.	£6 6s.	£7 10s.	£6 13s.

Much of the decline will be accounted for by a decline in the frequency with which old people are working. In the age group 65–69 about 40 per cent of the men and husbands in couples were working full or part-time; by the age of 75 and over, however, the percentage had fallen to 9 per cent for men and 16 per cent for couples. Women, as we have seen, were much less often in employment anyway, but the percentage who worked also declined from 19 per cent in the age group 65–69 to 4 per cent of those aged 75 and over.

But even the median income for those who were completely retired showed a small but consistent tendency to fall over the age groups, particularly for the couples where it declined from just over £7 a week in the age group 65–69 to £6 6s. in the age group over 75. This tendency is confirmed by an examination of the distribution of income of the retired in different age-groups (see Table 17).

The percentage in the very lowest income groups increased for men, women and couples alike, who were 75 and over, compared with those in the age group 65–69. But the increase was greatest for the couples, no less than 38 per cent of whom, aged 75 and over, had incomes below £6 a week, and very nearly two-thirds had incomes below £7 a week. This is another example of the importance of employment income for the couples. At the other end of the income distribution, the percentage in the higher income groups declined for all types of income unit as age increased.

There is no similar clear cut tendency for the ownership of assets to decline over the age groups. On the contrary here the pattern is one of considerable stability. This is somewhat surprising since the

TABLE 17

Percentage of retired elderly income units by age and by amount of total gross weekly money income; Britain 1962

Range of total gross weekly income £ per week	Age group			All retired
	65–69	70–74	75+	
Men				
Up to £3	13	11	18	15
£3 up to £4	23	32	27	27
£4 up to £5	15	19	17	17
£5 up to £6	12	11	15	13
£6 up to £8	15	11	7	10
£8 up to £10	10	6	2	5
£10 and over	6	4	5	5
No answer	6	6	8	7
Total percentage	100	100	100	100
(Number of cases)	(83)	(100)	(208)	(391)
Women				
Up to £3	20	23	28	25
£3 up to £4	32	38	35	35
£4 up to £5	19	17	18	18
£5 up to £6	8	6	8	7
£6 up to £8	6	6	3	5
£8 up to £10	3	2	1	2
£10 and over	5	2	1	2
No answer	7	5	7	6
Total percentage	100	100	100	100
(Number of cases)	(326)	(427)	(650)	(1,403)
Couples				
Up to £6	24	29	38	30
£6 up to £7	21	22	26	23
£7 up to £8	13	12	9	11
£8 up to £10	11	15	9	12
£10 up to £15	17	11	7	12
£15 and over	7	5	4	5
No answer	7	7	8	7
Total percentage	100	100	100	100
(Number of cases)	(273)	(247)	(250)	(770)

older people might have been expected to have used more of their savings. We have yet to complete our study of the light which the national survey throws upon older people's propensity to dissave. Over all age groups we find that 47 per cent of those with assets (or with no assets at the end of the year, but some at the beginning of the year) had drawn on them during the course of the year. There may be a group of old people who refuse to touch any money which they have put by. But on the basis of this evidence it is certainly not true of all old people. On the other hand although savings may be

TABLE 18

Percentage of all elderly income units by age with assets in the ranges stated; Britain 1962

Age group	Asset group					Total percentage (Number of cases)
	None	Less than £100	£100– £500	£500 or more	No answer	
Men						
65–69... ...	36	12	26	22	3	100 (141)
70–74... ...	30	16	22	31	1	100 (124)
75+	37	17	23	22	1 case	100 (230)
All	35	15	24	24	2	100 (495)
Women						
65–69... ...	35	16	21	26	2	100 (400)
70–74... ...	41	21	19	18	1	100 (477)
75+	45	17	19	18	1	100 (675)
All	41	18	20	20	1	100 (1,552)
Couples						
65–69... ...	28	14	30	26	2	100 (471)
70–74... ...	31	18	24	24	3	100 (332)
75+	30	19	22	26	3	100 (296)
All	30	16	26	25	2	100 (1,099)

run down during the course of retirement, the occasional windfall received in the form of a small legacy, or the small sum left to be put in the bank after paying the funeral expenses out of a burial policy, could all serve to counteract any average downward trend of assets with age. The forces at work producing these patterns of income and assets require further study.

In looking at cross-sectional data of this kind, however, some allowance must be made for the possible effect of differential mortality rates; and when considering the retired alone allowance must also be made for the possibility that the relatively better off may tend to retire earlier. On the other hand, since income from employers' pensions and items like rents tend to be relatively fixed in amount in a period of rising prices and incomes, this alone might explain why the older, who have been longer retired, have lower incomes.

One important fact does emerge. The older among the aged were certainly worse off than the younger both because of the operation of forces like inflation and because, as people got older they were less likely to be working. Because of the greater importance of employment for the men and couples in our sample, women tend to be more homogeneous in their financial position with respect to age than do the two former groups. In Table 19 we show the age distribution within quartiles of the income distribution. From this it can be seen that while 74 per cent of all the women were 70 or over, 81 per cent and 77 per cent in the lowest and second lowest quartile of the income distribution were 70 or over; and while 57 per cent of all the couples were 70 or over, 72 per cent and 74 per cent of the couples in the two lowest income quartiles were over 70.

TABLE 19
Percentage of elderly income units in each income quartile in each of three age groups; Britain 1962

Age group	Income quartile				
	Highest	2nd highest	2nd lowest	Lowest	All
Men... ...	£6 13s. and over	£4 12s. up to £6 13s.	£3 8s. up to £4 12s.	Up to £3 8s.	
65–69 ...	50	22	22	18	28
70–74 ...	24	26	31	21	26
75+... ...	25	51	47	61	47
Total ...	100	100	100	100	100
Women ...	£4 14s. and over	£3 14s. up to £4 14s.	£3 up to £3 14s.	Up to £3	
65–69 ...	36	25	23	20	26
70–74 ...	32	29	35	28	31
75+... ...	33	46	42	52	43
Total ...	100	100	100	100	100
Couples ...	£10 18s. and over	£7 10s. up to £10 18s.	£6 up to £7 10s.	Up to £6	
65–69 ...	59	50	36	28	43
70–74 ...	25	33	30	32	30
75+... ...	16	17	34	40	27
Total ...	100	100	100	100	100

The main problem group—women

"The women were worse off than couples or single and widowed men in every respect. They were less often working; fewer of them had private pensions; and although some of them had large amounts of assets, the majority—and again far more than men or couples—were without any at all or had only negligible sums."[1] This conclusion of the 1959–60 survey might be echoed in every respect as a description of our present findings.

At all ages the median income of the women was only a half that of the couples taking those in employment and the retired together. (See Table 16.) For the retired alone it was between 52 per cent and 54 per cent of the couples' income, when the level of the single person's retirement pension was 62 per cent of that of a man with a dependent wife. Almost a quarter of the women had incomes of less than £3 a week and only 6 per cent had incomes of £8 a week or more (or possibly 9 per cent to allow for the no answer cases). Indeed, the relative poverty of the women was underlined by expressing the intervals for our income distribution as percentages of the median income for each type of income unit separately. The top income group for women began at a point below the median income of the couples.

Although 36 per cent of the women were receiving national assistance compared with 16–20 per cent of the men and couples, this did not make up for their deficiency in respect of other sources of income. Perhaps one of the most remarkable contrasts was in the median level of women's employment income. Their full-time employment income was 50 per cent, their part-time employment income more than 60 per cent, below the couples. (See Table 12.) As many as a half of all the women had no income except their state income, and another 18 per cent had no more than £1 a week in addition. Altogether over *two-thirds of the women were solely or primarily dependent upon the state*. The evidence is overwhelming for regarding the single and widowed women as the major problem group among the elderly, both numerically (they form just under a half of all the income units over 65) and because of the paucity of their resources.

The women are not, of course, a completely homogeneous group. About a fifth have never been married; another fifth were widowed more than 20 years ago, and another fifth were widowed between 10 and 20 years ago. There was a suggestion in the survey material that the single women, and possibly the more recently widowed (i.e. those widowed less than 5 years ago), were a little better off than others. Certainly rather more of the single women had employers' pensions (18 per cent compared with 9 per cent of the widows), property income (33 per cent compared with 18 per cent of widows) and employment income (18 per cent compared with 9 per cent of widows). But even the single women did not come within reach of the men, financially speaking. It is possible that the financial position of the widow who lost her husband early on in marriage and who had no children would be more nearly like that of a single woman; and again, that there would be a difference between the financial position of women widowed before their husbands reached retirement age and those widowed afterwards. Such differences have not emerged from this

---

1. Cole, Dorothy with Utting, J., *op. cit.*, 1962, p. 102.

material but in any case they are likely to be small compared with the great difference which we have established as existing between the women and the men.

The differences are not due to sex as such, but to differences in employment experience, past and present. This is the dominant influence upon the financial position both of the man and the woman in old age (and here we speak of men not only as the single and widowed males of our income units, but also the husbands in couples). For women, however, the crucial factors are the absence of employment experience, or employment experience at levels of income which rarely rise above half those of their male counterparts.

CHAPTER 6

Living Alone and with Others; the Problems of
National Assistance and the Concept of 'Need'

How old people keep house

The discussion so far has concentrated upon the income and assets directly available to the old. But, it may be objected, this is misleading because an important element determining the standard of living which old people enjoy is the fact that many of them live with family and friends. At the very least they share the overheads of housekeeping like rent, rates and fuel, and many may receive additional help and subsidy.

Just under a half of all the units in the sample were keeping house with others (30 per cent of the couples, 55 per cent of the women and 63 per cent of the men).

TABLE 20

Ways of keeping house for those elderly people with incomes more than 5 per cent below the median income for their type of income unit; Britain 1962

	Men	Women	Couples
Total number of cases in the income groups more than 5 per cent below the median	208	628	472
Percentage in those income groups keeping house with relatives	% 62	% 64	% 28

In Chapter 4 of this section we concentrated upon those elderly people with incomes more than 5 per cent below the median for their type of income unit as having very low levels of income. As Table 20 shows, relatively more of the women in these lowest income groups were sharing house than were all women. In part, this is the effect of national assistance. Old people on their own with national assistance will almost certainly receive a higher average weekly allowance than those living with others (but also receiving assistance) because the former will receive a full rent allowance, whereas old people sharing, will, if they are householders in the national assistance sense, be assumed to receive a reasonable contribution towards the rent from the other member, or members, of the household; and if they are not householders will be assessed on a rather lower scale, the rent allowance being restricted similarly to a share of the household rent

111

Even when units receiving national assistance are excluded from the picture altogether sharing is still more common in the lowest income groups among the men and the women. For couples there is little difference. In the income groups more than 5 per cent below the median and without national assistance, 74 per cent of the men and 71 per cent of the women were sharing house. Among men sharing and not receiving national assistance nearly a third had incomes below £3 12s. a week; among men alone the figure is 20 per cent. Among women sharing and not receiving national assistance 40 per cent had incomes below £2 19s. a week (most of these women had no income but the retirement pension) and 50 per cent had incomes below £3 10s.[1] Among women alone the figures were 21 per cent and 32 per cent.

Differences in housing expenditure for those sharing and those alone can be allowed for in comparing their financial resources. We have subtracted this item of expenditure from total weekly income and compared the median of the income then remaining for units sharing house and for those living alone.[2]

TABLE 21

Median total weekly income after meeting housing expenses of those units sharing house and those living alone; Britain 1962

| Type of income unit | Median weekly income of units sharing a home with | | Alone |
| | Relatives | Non-relatives | |
	£ per week		
Men	£3 10s.	£5 10s.	£4 0s.
Women	£2 17s.	£3 12s.	£3 2s.
Couples*			
(i) Wife under 60	£6 18s.	Only 2 cases	£8 11s.
(ii) Wife 60 and over ...	£6 5s.	Only 13 cases	£6 9s.

* This distinction between wives under 60 and 60 and over was made for cross-national purposes

The differences in income remaining to those living alone and those living with relatives were very similar to the differences in the scale rates allowed by the National Assistance Board to householders and non-householders.[3] Those living alone had only a few shillings more a week with one exception, which was couples with wives under 60. Finding that more of the old at the bottom of the income distribution were sharing house, helps to explain why, with the income and asset levels revealed by this survey, there was not more obvious

1. These are the median income groupings (see Table 3, p. 83).
2. The figure of housing expenditure is what the old person told us was paid for the accommodation. Even where they were living with others this would sometimes be the whole rent or rates because the old person was the tenant/owner. In these cases no allowance has been made for contributions to the rent from the rest of the household. Sometimes the old person would say 'nothing' because they did not make a specific earmarked contribution to the housing expenditure which was the responsibility of another member of the household. In these cases no allowance has been made for the fact that the old person may well have paid a share of the rent.
3. See above p. 86.

hardship among old people. But how relevant this fact of sharing is to questions of 'need' and to discussions about the adequacy of levels of state benefits is a complicated matter.

First, it should not be assumed that all old people who are sharing are doing so with well-off sons and daughters. The present survey did not attempt to assess the financial position of the members of the household not over 65. But an examination of the relationship between the old person and the rest of the household is itself very revealing.

TABLE 22

The marital status of elderly individuals keeping house in different ways;[1] Britain 1962

Ways of keeping house	Single and widowed males	Single and widowed females	All married males and females
Living alone or with spouse only ...	36	45	68
Living with others of whom: ...	64	55	32
living with married child	36	32	14
living with unmarried child ...	27	34	68
living with siblings	18	20	6
living with other relatives	6	5	7
other non-relatives	13	9	5
Total percentage	100	100	100

From Table 22 we see that although the majority of old people sharing were sharing with a child, in many cases this was with an unmarried child. Over a quarter of the men, a third of the women and well over two-thirds of the married people who were sharing, were doing so with an unmarried child; of these more than a half were living with an unmarried daughter. Another significant group, among the men and women at least, were living with siblings, often themselves old age pensioners. Finally from 12 per cent (married people) to 19 per cent (men) were living with other more distant relatives or with non-relatives. In most cases the other members of the household will be income-receivers (although examples of old people caring for illegitimate grandchildren or for handicapped children of their own can be given), and the advantages of the sharing of house-hold overheads will accrue. But it would be dangerous to make sweeping assumptions about the extent of other forms of subsidy to the old from members of the household who may themselves have low incomes, or may not even be related to the old person at all.

Operations of the National Assistance Board

What is the National Assistance Board's present approach to this problem and what effect does it have upon the income levels of

---

1. These data relate to individuals not income units.

the old? We have seen that the National Assistance Board lays down scale rates as a measure of 'need' for everything excluding rent and needs arising from 'special circumstances'.

The National Assistance Board's criteria are the contemporary administrative definition of financial 'need'. Historically these criteria derive from the work of Beveridge and Rowntree, in that when national assistance first came into operation in 1948 the scale rates were then set at levels roughly equivalent, in real terms, to the pre-war Rowntree Human Needs Standard as revised by Beveridge. Since then scale rates have been increased in real terms but only on the basis of statements about 'sharing in prosperity'. Whether there is any more objective attempt to calculate needs has not been made public.

The scale rate for couples does not differ whether they are house-holders or not; the only effect which sharing a household has upon their position is that if they are paying the rent they are assumed to receive a reasonable contribution towards it from the other members, or to pay a reasonable contribution if someone else is the householder. In the case of one person (men and women), the reasonable contri-bution to others or from others, for the rent, is also assumed, but in addition, as we have seen, the scale rate for 'non-householder' is a few shillings a week lower than that for the 'householder'. This is a flat rate difference applied to all, and turning only upon the applica-tion of the definition of householder by the Board's officers. Besides administering the scale rates, however, the National Assistance Board has discretionary power to make additions to those scale rates (to anyone, householder or non-householder), for 'special needs'. These special needs are decided upon after investigation of individual cir-cumstances. Grants are made for such things as special diets, extra fuel and laundry. Finally, the Board has powers to make grants for 'exceptional needs' which are once and for all payments.[1] Again these are needs decided upon in the light of an investigation of any individual's circumstances.

In the determination of entitlement to a weekly allowance the Board can only take account of the financial resources of the applicant with power to disregard certain amounts and kinds of income and of assets.[2] In making discretionary payments and grants for exceptional needs the 'individual circumstances' which are taken into account are less easily defined. Presumably account will be taken of the stocks of clothing and household items already in the possession of the old person. In the case of old people sharing house, the Board is not allowed to investigate or take direct account of the means of the other

---

1. For example see *Report of the National Assistance Board* 1962 *and* 1963, Cmnd 2078, p. 32 and Cmnd 2386, p. 31 London, HMSO.
2. For details see *Annual Report of the National Assistance Board* 1959, Cmnd 1085, p. 17–18 (Lon-don, HMSO. Broadly, income from employers' pensions, trade unions, allowances from rela-tives, etc., is disregarded up to 15s. a week; war disability pensions and industrial injury benefit up to 30s.; and earnings up to a maximum of 30s. plus half the next 20s. Capital up to £125 (£375 if in 'war' savings) is disregarded completely and the limit of capital above which assistance is not payable is £600. Between £125 and £600 capital is taken into account at the rate of 6d. a week for the first £125 and each subsequent £25.

members of the household; although as has been stated, these other members are expected to make their proper contribution to the rent if the old person is a householder. But it is not at all clear how the general appearance of comfort, or otherwise, of the other members of the household will influence the Board's decision to make or to withhold a grant for exceptional needs.

As far as weekly payments from the Board are concerned they are certainly not confined to those living alone. In our sample 43 per cent of all the income units receiving national assistance were sharing house (compared with 50 per cent of those not receiving national assistance). This appears high when compared with the National Assistance Board's own figure of 32 per cent. Their figures do include women between 60 and 64 among whom there may be a relatively greater tendency to be living alone, but it is unlikely to explain all the difference.[1] The Board's reports do not say how many discretionary additions or grants for exceptional need go to old people sharing house (they have been asked to provide this information) but there must be quite a number. Discretionary additions have almost ceased to be 'special' for old people. In 1963, 68 per cent of all retirement pensioners with weekly allowances were receiving discretionary additions and they averaged 8s. 10d. a week.

In 1963 a total of 314,000 grants for 'exceptional need' were made to all classes of recipient of national assistance (not just pensioners) at a time when there were nearly 2 million weekly allowances in payment.[2] We do not know how many went to the aged. We do know that in our sample only 4 per cent of those receiving national assistance reported receiving such a grant for exceptional need in the preceding year. This figure should perhaps be treated with caution because of difficulties of memory over such a long period but they are clearly relatively infrequent. Most grants of this kind to the elderly appear to be to replace bedding or clothes. But even allowing for understatement, the percentage seems low in the light of likely need, in view of what we know about stocks of clothing and bedding possessed by old people.[3]

The present system of defining 'need' then, is in the main an impersonal one of laying down overall regulations for matching resources of income and assets against specified 'needs' which vary only with the rent paid and the position in the household. There is not a household means test. But it can also be in part, a personal definition of need in respect of discretionary additions. It is impossible to say in the operation of this part, how much weight, if any, is given to the financial position of the rest of the household.

One interesting feature, in part the consequence of the present

---

1. Cmnd 2386, *op. cit.*, Appendix X.
2. Cmnd 2386, *op, cit.* Table 9 and p. 31.
3. Wedderburn, Dorothy Cole, *op. cit.*, 1962, p. 279. Evidence from the 1959–60 survey was there quoted showing that of women living alone with incomes of less than £8 a week, a fifth possessed a minimum or less in respect of two household items like blankets, sheets, etc., and 31 per cent in respect of one essential item of clothing.

system of defining 'need' for national assistance, is the discovery that the recipients of national assistance are not all to be found with incomes heavily concentrated around the scale rates. Even after the deduction of rent, there appears to be a considerable spread of income as a result of the operation of disregards (which, of course, have little to do with 'need' but reflect, in general, the desire to administer a means test in such a way as not to remove all incentive to 'self-help'), and of the discretionary additions.

The distribution of income for those with national assistance

It is a pity that the Board do not themselves publish data on the distribution of total weekly income (before and after paying rent) available to the most important categories of their recipients. Our material only allows us to give very approximate figures of this kind for two reasons. The first is our treatment of housing expenditure which in cases where old people are sharing house, we know will not necessarily coincide with the Board's treatment. The second is that our definition of householder is very arbitrary and may also differ from that of the Board. However, total weekly income after deduction of housing expenditure for all people in the sample receiving national assistance was matched against the scale rate appropriate to their position as householder or non-householder as defined by the survey, and against the scale rate ruling at the time of their interview.[1]

TABLE 23

The percentage of elderly income units receiving national assistance having total weekly income minus housing expenditure in the ranges stated around the level of national assistance scale rates; Britain 1962

From below scale rate to 5 per cent above	5 per cent up to 15 per cent above	15 per cent up to 40 per cent above	40 per cent up to 60 per cent above	60 per cent and over	No answer
36	23	27	6	5	3

The intervals chosen around the scale rate are quite arbitrary. Fifteen per cent above, represents 8s. above the single householder's, and approximately 15s. above a couple's scale rate at the time of the first interviews. It seemed a reasonable interval to take in order to include people with some discretionary additions to their weekly allowance, or with a small amount of disregarded income. Forty per cent above the scale rate represents a little over £1 a week on top of the single householder's, and £1 15s. a week on top of the couple's scale rate.

Of the 36 per cent of all units shown in Table 23 to be receiving national assistance and to have incomes at or below the scale rate, 23 per cent actually fell below the scale rate. These cases have been

1. Scale rates were increased between the first and second stages of interviewing. See above p. 84.

examined with some care, because a recipient of national assistance would not be expected to be in this position. Most cases result from the rounding down (when converting to whole shillings in the analysis) of amounts of income received, so that small variations from the scale rate must be ignored; others occur in cases where the definition of householder or of rent payment could well differ from that of the National Assistance Board. But 4 per cent of all the cases with national assistance fell a good way below the scale rate and a satisfactory explanation is not yet available. This fact should be borne in mind when interpreting the data. In Table 23 we have shown men, women and couples together; but the pattern is very similar for all three types of income unit. In general the majority of old people with national assistance do appear to be receiving incomes above the bare scale rate. In the first place this should be seen as a tribute to the flexibility with which the system is administered.

In view of this, however, it would not be altogether surprising to find quite large numbers of old people without national assistance but who were not significantly better off than those with national assistance. A number of reasons could account for this. If they happened to have resources a little above the scale rates, but then they were to develop special needs for diet or some other requirement they might well not think of applying to the National Assistance Board; or if they did have entitlement but were proud or ignorant they simply might not apply; or if they happened to have the type of resources which cannot be disregarded by the Board they could be excluded from entitlement.

'Need' among those without national assistance

In exactly the same way as for those with national assistance the income of those without national assistance, after deduction for rent, was matched against the appropriate national assistance scale rate. In order to approach National Assistance Board criteria more closely, assets were also brought into the picture. It must be stressed that this is in no sense a calculation of the number of people in our sample who had entitlement to national assistance. The information is not available for such a calculation to be made. The difficulties involved in defining 'householders' and 'rent' have already been touched upon. Moreover in this calculation no allowance has been made for income or capital which might be disregarded, nor for special needs. The analysis simply enables us to compare the financial resources available to the old with and without national assistance, making the same very rough and ready allowance for the differences of need occasioned by levels of rent and household sharing for both groups.

There were 11 per cent of all units in the sample who were without national assistance whose income, as defined, was no more than 5 per cent above the appropriate scale rate and who had no assets or less than £500. Of these, 5 per cent were living quite alone and 6 per cent were sharing house. At levels between the appropriate scale rate and not more than 15 per cent above it (again with assets of

TABLE 24

The percentage of all elderly income units who were not receiving national assistance having total weekly income minus housing expenditure and assets in the ranges stated around national assistance scale rates; Britain 1962

Income level in relation to scale rates	Living alone	With others
Below up to 5 per cent above		
with assets below £500	5	6
with assets £500+	2	1
5 per cent above up to 15 per cent		
with assets below £500	2	5
with assets £500+	1	1
15 per cent above up to 40 per cent		
with assets below £500	3	3
with assets £500+	1	1
40 per cent above up to 60 per cent		
with assets below £500	2	2
with assets £500+	1	1
60 per cent above up to 100 per cent		
with assets below £500	4	3
with assets £500+	2	1
100 per cent and above		
with assets below £500	5	5
with assets £500+	5	3
No answer		
with assets below £500	2	2
with assets £500+	2	2
Total as percentage of all units (including those with national assistance) in the sample, i.e. 3,146 ...	37	36

less than £500), another 2 per cent were living alone, and 5 per cent were living with others.[1]   But in Table 23 we saw that more than a quarter of the people with national assistance had incomes between 15 per cent and 40 per cent above the scale rate.   Looking at those without national assistance we find that those of them who, too, had incomes 15 per cent to 40 per cent above the scale rate represented another 6 per cent of the total sample.   Altogether then, 24 per cent of the sample, nearly as many people again as were receiving national assistance, had financial resources not significantly higher than those who were receiving national assistance.

At the risk of labouring the point we must repeat why these figures do not tell us about entitlement to national assistance.   In examining the financial resources of both groups—those with national assistance and those without—the same standards to allow for variations in rent, and in sharing house have been applied.   But these are not precisely the same standards as the National Assistance Board itself uses.   In some respects they are more stringent (for instance there is no allowance for disregarding certain kinds of resources) and

---

1.   All these percentages have been calculated on the assumption that the 'no answer' cases have resources higher than those specified here.

in some respects they are more generous (for instance there is no allowance for contributions from other members of the household to the rent). On balance we believe that they are criteria roughly comparable to national assistance criteria; and if the latter may be regarded as criteria for defining a contemporary subsistence standard we may then speak of the numbers of old people at subsistence levels found in our sample.

It is probably not an exaggeration then to say that the 11 per cent of all units in the sample without national assistance but with resources below scale rate levels were 'poor' by any standards (although not necessarily all 'in poverty' because some were keeping house with other people). Another 13 per cent were above the minimum standard but still at levels of income no higher than those achieved by many who do receive national assistance. It could be argued that some of the variety in income level of those with assistance reflects the payment of discretionary additions which cover 'special needs' and which do not exist among the old without national assistance; to use the resulting income levels as criteria of general need is then misleading. More evidence is badly needed here for it is by no means obvious that such special needs do not exist among the group without national assistance.

But taking those in the sample with national assistance, and those without but with similar levels of financial resources together, the evidence points to one half of all old people over 65 having resources in their own right very close to contemporary subsistence levels. The position of particular individuals may differ, but clearly there will be a good deal of overlap between this group and that half of the sample who we found to be solely or primarily dependent on state benefits.[1]

Some readers may object that this analysis still does not take sufficient account of the help which comes from sharing house. But to do so would be to invite some form of household means test and involves many value judgments which we discuss below.[2] But what of those old people with and without national assistance who are living alone. What does a contemporary subsistence level mean for them in terms of living standards?

The expenditure of old people and the concept of 'need'

In the national survey we could not attempt to collect expenditure information. But the 1962 Family Expenditure Survey of the Ministry of Labour covers the same period as our income and asset data. An analysis of the expenditure patterns of households where the head was 'retired or unoccupied' has been published.[3] This certainly casts some light on the levels of living achieved by the old in different income groups. The most interesting information from the viewpoint of the present discussion is summarised in Table 25, p. 121. The lowest income

1. See above p. 96.
2. See below p. 127.
3. *Family Expenditure Survey* 1962, Table 6, London, HMSO.

119

group (up to £4 a week) comprises households which, judging from the average number of persons per household, must nearly all contain only one person, and can therefore be regarded as approximating very closely indeed to our men and women with income below the median incomes of £4 11s. and £3 14s. a week. The income group in the Ministry of Labour data which contains mostly two person households, £6 but under £10 a week, does not correspond so well to our couples with incomes below their median (£7 10s. a week), but it may serve as a rough guide. As an indication of how far these two groups represent the poorest among the old in 1962 we may note that total expenditure minus housing in the lowest income group was between 20 and 30 per cent above the 1962 national assistance scale rate for a single person, but in the income group £6 but under £10, total expenditure minus housing was between 60 and 70 per cent above the scale rate for a couple.

One technical point should be noted. Average total weekly expenditure of every income group in Table 25 exceeds average total weekly income by amounts varying from 17 to 29 per cent of income. Some of the difference may be accounted for by dis-saving; but most of it will be the result of phenomena which occur in the lower income groups in all budget studies. This is no place to discuss the reasons for such a discrepancy except to note that it is probably the result of a combination of factors; first, a statistical phenomenon arising from grouping data which are subject to random errors of observation; second, some, although probably relatively little, understatement of income; third to the omission from the Family Expenditure Survey income definition of windfall items including maturing insurance policies, occasional money gifts, etc.; fourth, to some overstatement of expenditure on certain items (enough to outweigh probable understatement of expenditure on alcohol, tobacco and cigarettes).[1] The point which concerns us here is that the recorded levels of expenditure all exceed what would be possible without dis-saving if the level of income is as stated.

The major item of expenditure is food, and per capita expenditure is fairly stable over the income groups. The data appear consistent with the figures from the National Food Survey for pensioner households which show a marked improvement in food consumption by pensioners over the period 1956 to 1961.[2] In his essay on the National Food Survey Dr Royston Lambert has this to say: ". . . until more general evidence is forthcoming to the contrary the general rise in the nutritional status of pensioners *as a single group* [his italics] must be accepted as the most satisfactory fact revealed by the dietary standard in this period".[3] Translated very roughly into quantities,

---

1. For a discussion of these methodological problems see Cole, Dorothy and Utting, J., "Estimating Expenditure Saving and Income from Household Budget Surveys", *Journal of the Royal Statistical Society*, Series A, Vol. 119, Part IV; also Appendix VII of *Family Expenditure Surv y* 1962, *op. cit.*
2. *Domestic Food Consumption and Expenditure:* 1961, para. 47. Ministry of Agriculture, Fisheries and Food, London, HMSO.
3. Lambert, R., *Nutrition in Britain* 1950–60, Occasional Papers on Social Administration No. 6, Codicote Press, Welwyn, 1964.

TABLE 25

Expenditure in 1962 of households with either retired or unoccupied heads

	Weekly income of household		
	Under £4	£4 but under £6	£6 but under £10
Number of households	129	190	208
Number of persons per household	1·02	1·39	1·97
	s. d.	s. d.	s. d.
Average weekly household income ...	67 2	99 2	154 2
Average weekly expenditure on:			
Housing	17 8	21 10	28 6
Fuel and light	13 0	16 7	20 3
Food	31 6	42 8	63 10
Alcohol	0 7	2 2	4 5
Tobacco	2 0	4 6	8 3
Clothing	6 5	4 8	11 11
Durable household goods...	2 4	4 3	6 2
Other goods	5 11	7 8	13 6
Transport, etc.	1 8	3 4	8 6
Services	5 8	8 2	17 1
Total above expenditure	86 9	115 9	182 6

the Ministry of Labour figures would suggest that the average old person living alone in the lowest income group could, in 1962, have been buying, each week, about one pound of carcase meat and another pound or so of bacon, cooked meats, etc. He or she could have bought four eggs, five pints of milk and half a pound of butter. Nearly 2s. a week would have gone on tea, 5s. a week on bread, cakes, biscuits, 1s. a week on potatoes, 2s. on other vegetables but only 1s. 6d. a week on fresh fruit—which in 1962 might have bought a pound of apples and an orange.

These quantities, and their translation into nutrient content, do confirm the impression that even in the lowest income groups today, money alone does not prevent an old person from having an adequate diet with some variety, provided food expenditure has a certain priority.[1] But if there are physical or other difficulties which hamper shopping or cooking; or if the old person has other priorities—such as those of the old lady who clung to renting her television set because it was almost her only contact with the outside world and her only entertainment—then the threshold of malnutrition may easily be approached.

Fuel expenditure was on average 13s. per week in the lowest income group. In 1962 the winter price of the grade 3 coal was on average 11s. 8d. a hundredweight, so that, allowing for some expenditure on gas and electricity out of the total of fuel expenditure it seems that probably not much more than one hundredweight of coal was being purchased each week for nine months of the year. This is

---

1. That is adequate by standards based on the recommendations of the BMA. For criticisms of those standards see Lambert, *op. cit.*, 1964.

not a very generous supply for old people home all day. In this lowest income group, average expenditure on the necessities of food, fuel and housing accounted for a total of £3 2s. a week. One of the interesting facts brought out by the detailed Ministry of Labour figures is how other items of expenditure, small in themselves and certainly regarded as essential at higher standards of living, soon total to a not inconsiderable sum when measured against this figure. Soaps and cleaning materials average 1s. 8d. a week; newspapers 1s. 10d.; laundry, cleaning, shoe repairs 1s. 4d.; radio and television licences and rental 1s. 6d. and bus fares 1s. 2d.; altogether, another 7s. 6d. week. At the sort of levels of income which so many of the men and women in our sample received, it is clear that once these basic items had been bought there would be little margin left for expenditure on clothing or on household goods. Moreover the averages conceal the real difficulties experienced by individual households in weeks in which for instance, the television licence, or a large shoe repair bill, had to be paid.

The couples were probably relatively better off, not only because their income, even on a per capita basis was higher than that of the single women at least, but also because, as Table 25 shows, expenditure on household overheads like housing and fuel and light does not increase pro rata with the increase in the number of people in the household. On the other hand, men are more likely than old ladies to feel the need for a smoke or a pint of beer, and two packets of cigarettes a week in 1962 would have cost 7s. The recorded expenditure on tobacco in the top income group in Table 25 was 8s. 3d. and this may have understated a little what was actually spent, assuming that like everyone else the old also understate expenditure on this item.[1]

Further study of existing expenditure data relating to old people —for instance an analysis of the Ministry of Labour data for households consisting only of one or two old people—would be extremely useful as a beginning to providing the necessary information upon which judgments might be based about 'needs' and the adequacy or otherwise of state benefits. Without such study it is all too easy to make sweeping and misleading assumptions. In a brief note, also using the Family Expenditure data over the two years ended June 1962, Dr Mark Abrams showed that the per capita expenditure of 'special pensioner households' expressed as a percentage of per capita expenditure of all households sampled, varied widely according to the type of commodity being considered.[2] Overall the total expenditure of special pensioner households including mortgage payments was 65 per cent of the corresponding total for all households. For items like transport and vehicles the per capita expenditure of the special pensioner households was only 15 per cent of the average for all households; for durable household goods 26 per cent, clothing 38

1. See *Family Expenditure Survey, op. cit.*, p. 89.
2. Abrams, M., "The Family Expenditure Survey and Old People", *Quarterly Bulletin of the National Old People's Welfare Council*, No. 61. "Special pensioners households" are defined by the Ministry of Labour as households in which three-quarters or more of total income is derived from National Insurance retirement or similar pensions and/or national assistance.

per cent; for miscellaneous goods 38 per cent and miscellaneous services 44 per cent. But for housing it was 95 per cent and for fuel 147 per cent. Dr Abrams comments:

> Many of these differences are logical enough, the small Special Pensioner household is not able to reduce proportionately its expenditure on rent and fuel; and old age pensioners normally have little need to buy new furniture and domestic equipment. Probably their greatest relative deprivation lies in the consumption of what are described in the statistics as miscellaneous goods and miscellaneous services.

Even if we are prepared to accept the view that the old age pensioner has little need to buy certain kinds of major domestic equipment, it is unlikely that pensioners with an average expectation of life of from ten to fifteen years are never going to need to replace curtains, chair covers, sheets or tea towels. All of these items fall under the Ministry of Labour heading of 'durable household goods'. But one could take issue with Dr Abrams on other grounds. If we consider 'need' alone, a better case can be made for certain old people to be equipped with major items of domestic equipment than for some younger people. Those of the elderly who have shopping difficulties 'need' a refrigerator more than those who can get easily to the shops. Those who are ailing or have become too frail, 'need' the help of washing machines. Those who are immobile or isolated 'need' a television to bring some entertainment and relief into their lives. But if older people do not enter the period of retirement already owners of these durable items the purchase of them out of income is largely out of the question.

To summarise the present discussion, there is at least a *prima facie* case for saying that old people living alone at the subsistence levels described in this survey, are today 'relatively deprived' in respect of all but a rather narrow range of conventional necessities.

123

CHAPTER 7

Income Security: Conclusions and Discussion

The national findings and other evidence

There are four important points to emerge from this discussion of the findings of the 1962 national survey. First, there is the evidence of the overwhelming importance of state income for the elderly, despite the existence of other sources of income in old age. A half of all the income units in the sample were primarily dependent upon state income. Second, there is the evidence of the gulf which exists financially between the 10 per cent of older people who continue to work full-time and those of the elderly who are retired. Third, there is the identification of the characteristics which have been found to be particularly associated with low financial resources. They are sex and age. The single and widowed women are worse off in every respect than are the single and widowed men or couples. But the older age groups among men, women and couples are all worse off than their younger counterparts, not only because they are less often working but because their other sources of income are lower too. On the other hand, although explored less fully, the survey suggests that perhaps a fifth of all old people (nearly 1 million income units in the population) were relatively 'well off'. That is, 'well off' judged by the standards by which the finances of the old have been measured in this analysis; compared with the community generally they might be judged to be not more than, or even below, average. The characteristics of those with the higher levels of financial resources were that they were either people still in employment or combining two or three modest sources of income.

The discussion of 'needs' provoked two observations. First, we looked at the kind of living standards achieved by the elderly living alone with incomes at the 1962 national assistance levels. There it appeared that the 'necessities' of life—food, housing, fuel—were being met at a not too stringent level of consumption; but that in respect of a wide range of other commodities, which many sections of the community would certainly regard as necessities, the elderly were relatively deprived. Second, we found that as many as 11 per cent of our sample had financial resources actually below national assistance scale rates, although they were not receiving national assistance. This was not a calculation about entitlement to national assistance and as the regulations stand such old people would not necessarily be entitled. But the financial resources of this group were clearly minimal. Then there were another 13 per cent of income units at or above the scale rates but with resources no higher than those units receiving national assistance. Altogether, taking those with and without national assistance, it appears that nearly a half of all elderly income units have financial resources at the current administratively defined 'subsistence' levels.

This was also the conclusion reached by the 1959–60 survey. Those who felt that that survey understated the financial resources available to older people will receive small comfort from the present inquiry. Between the dates of the two surveys the retirement pension had been increased by 7s. 6d. a week for a single person and 12s. 6d. for a couple; and national assistance scale rates by 3s. 6d. for a single householder and 5s. 0d. for a couple by the time of the first stage of interviewing in the national survey, and by 7s. 6d. and 10s. 6d. by the second stage. Allowing for this, Table 26 shows marked agreement between the two surveys as to the general shape of the income distribution, particularly if the 'no answer' cases in the national survey data are assumed all to belong to the income groups over £6 a week single or £9 a week couples.

TABLE 26

Percentage of all elderly income units with total gross weekly money income in the ranges stated in the 1959/60 and 1962 national surveys compared

Range of total gross weekly income £ per week	Men		Women		Couples	
	1959/60	Britain 1962	1959/60	Britain 1962	1959/60	Britain 1962
No income and up to £3	17	13	32	23	—	⎫
£3 up to £4 ...	30	23	31	33	—	⎬ 8
£4 up to £5 ...	15	15	13	18	12	⎭
£5 up to £6 ...	7	12	8	8	21	16
£6 up to £8 ...	13	11	6	6	22	28
£8 up to £10 ...	3	7	3	2	13	14
£10 up to £15 ...	7	6	3	2	14	17
£15 up to £20 ...	1	3	2	1	7	6
£20 and over ...	7	2	2	1	10	5
No answer	—	8	—	6	—	7
Total percentage ...	100	100	100	100	100	100
Number of cases ...	141	495	607	1,552	298	1,099
Median income ...	£4 8s.	£4 11s.	£3 10s.	£3 14s.	£7 10s.	£7 10s.

Entitled to national assistance but not receiving it

In the present national survey the information collected was not detailed enough, nor analysed in a way which enabled us to investigate whether there were older people with entitlement to national assistance and not receiving it. We could only compare financial levels in broad terms with scale rates.[1] But the question of entitlement was investigated

1. See above p. 117.

in some detail in the 1959–60 survey. It was estimated that some 9–11 per cent of all elderly income units had entitlement but were without assistance.[1] In view of the general agreement in the overall findings of the two surveys and the stability of the percentage of retirement pensioners receiving national assistance over the period 1959 to 1962, as shown by official figures, the percentage is probably still around that figure. This would represent about half a million income units in the total population.

Confirmation of this estimate has recently come from another quarter. In its study of the impact of rates on households, the Allen Committee made a special study of households with low financial resources. Households with retired heads were treated as a special group. The Committee concluded that:

> Despite the qualifications and reservations that need to be made about our data on resources of the special study households, it appears that an appreciable percentage of households *with retired heads are eligible for national assistance but are not getting it* [our italics].

The Committee's survey data showed some 800,000 households in this category, but after making some allowance for understatement of resources they arrive at: '... a figure of half a million for the number of retired householders apparently eligible for assistance but not getting it'.[2] The Ministry of Pensions is now conducting its own inquiry into this problem and its results are awaited with great interest.[3]

It would, of course, be encouraging to find that our estimates and those of the Allen Committee were too high. But it is, in any case, misleading to concentrate too much upon the question of entitlement. What matters more than entitlement, under the regulations as they now stand, is the actual level of financial resources available to the old; and no more evidence is required before we can conclude that there are very many old people *without* national assistance but who are little better off than those old people who do receive national assistance.

Changes since 1962

Bearing in mind what the levels of national assistance scale rates were in the latter part of 1962—that is £2 17s. 6d. a week for a single householder and £4 15s. 6d. for a couple—we might conclude that certain important financial needs of older people were failing to be met. How far has the picture changed since then? National assistance scale rates increased 30 per cent in money terms between 1962 and March 1965; the retirement pension increased 40 per cent.[4] Some of these increases were eroded by rising prices. If a special

---

1. Cole, Dorothy with Utting, J., *op. cit.*, 1962, p. 101, gave a figure of 12 per cent or 11 per cent after allowing for bias. The full sample gives a figure of 9 per cent.
2. Cmnd 2582, *op. cit.*, pp. 224–225.
3. See above, p. 76.
4. See Table 4, p. 86.

pensioner index were available it would probably show a rise of some 11 per cent (compared with the 9 per cent rise of the official retail price index) over the period January 1962 to December 1964.[1] In round terms elderly people receiving state benefits have probably had a real increase in their income levels of between 20 and 30 per cent over the last two to two and a half years; that is, a bigger increase than other incomes generally. While such an improvement is very welcome, as the comparison in Chapter 4 showed, it will go only a small way towards reducing the gap which exists between the standard of living available to the elderly and other sections of society. Before we can decide on reasonable contemporary definitions of 'need' more information must be obtained about the socially acceptable minimum levels of expenditure today on those items where the old are relatively deprived, like clothes, household goods and services of all kinds. In particular this information must be analysed in relation to the problems of living for long periods of time upon low levels of income, for this is the expectation of most old people when they retire. What may be an acceptable 'minimum income' for the short period of an emergency is not necessarily acceptable for ten or fifteen years.

One important dimension of a study of the economic problems of old age has been left for exploration in later publications. That is the inter-relationship between the financial and other problems of the aged. This is an essential aspect of the 1962 national survey. A small beginning has been made in Chapter 1 of Part I and it is already possible to say that many of the poorest, in financial terms, are also those with some of the most serious problems of health and of self-care. Certainly what we have seen of the association between employment status and income level, and between age and income level, would lead us to expect this.

Policy implications

The full material in this survey will yield much of value for those responsible for the framing of pension policy. From the present analysis three broad areas emerge as requiring attention if we are to develop a rational system of social security in old age. The first is the problem of 'need' and the ways in which old people keep house. The second is the various administrative devices which are at present canvassed by the political parties for identifying those whose need is greatest.[2] These are problems of today's pensioners. The third is a brief comment on the shape of state schemes for future pensioners.

(i) *Need and the household means test* The data have shown how we may reconcile the views of those who, on the one hand, speak of the poverty which must result from the low level of the retirement pension, and of those on the other hand who say that evidence of acute poverty or dire hardship among the old is lacking.[3] Many of the poorest

---

1. A rough calculation using weights from the Family Expenditure data reproduced in Table 25.
2. See above p. 75.
3. See, for instance, *Hansard*, 9th July 1964.

are in fact living with children or other relatives. But the data also warn against over-facile assumptions about the financial resources of the children or relatives in such circumstances. Moreover it must be remembered that the survey did not produce systematic evidence on a point which is widely considered to be important by many workers in this field. That is the psychological 'need' for economic independence among old people who are sharing house. Such old people often have a strong desire to avoid being an economic as well as, possibly, a physical burden.

Leaving such considerations aside however, there appears to be some confusion about exactly what weight is at present given to the economic position of the rest of the household in the administration of the means test through national assistance. For instance, in commenting on the Labour Party's proposals for an 'income guarantee' administered through an Income Tax return, Mr Boyd Carpenter said:

> The point I was putting to the House is the difficulty of judging the needs of a person on income alone, which is the only thing which the income tax returns will give. One can take the case of two people, one a retired pensioner with a plentiful stock of clothes living with a younger relative in a comfortable house. The other is the old lady living by herself with the stock of clothes nearly exhausted and paying a high rent. Under a scheme turning on the Income Tax return it is not possible, as I understand it, to distinguish between the two because only income, not needs, is taken into account.[1]

In referring to the 'comfortable house' he was suggesting a far more comprehensive test of means than the regulations of the National Assistance Board provide, certainly in deciding on whether or not to grant a weekly allowance, and probably also in deciding on whether or not to grant a discretionary addition.[2]

In the actual administration of the test of means and definition of needs in this country, since 1941, the trend has theoretically been away from the 'household means test'.[3] Any line drawn to define resources is bound to be an arbitrary one, and it will reflect social judgments. But it should be recognised that those who attach great importance to this form of inter-household subsidy from children when judging the adequacy of the present levels of state benefits, are, by implication, suggesting a reversal of the trend which has tended to restrict the definition of resources to those which are available to the individual as of right.

(ii) *Identifying those who need help most* The policy makers are faced with the difficulty of reconciling two objectives. On the one

1. *Hansard*, 10th December 1963, Col. 341.
2. See above p. 114.
3. See *National Assistance Board Report*, 1948, Cmnd 7767, London, HMSO. As recently as 1959 there was a further move away from the household means test when the 'assumed contribution' of 7s. a week from an earning member of the household to the householder in receipt of national assistance was abolished. But it can be argued that the household means test may have been brought in through the back door with the increasing importance of discretionary allowances.

hand to limit the size of the pensions bill, on the other hand to avoid, if possible, the use of a means test because of public opposition to any support which smacks of 'charity'. The evidence presented here of the extent to which older people with entitlement to national assistance still do not apply, shows how widespread is the dislike of a means test where individuals have to go and ask for help. Both of these objectives—limiting expenditure on pensions and avoiding a means test—already imply the adoption of certain priorities.

The earnings rule is a device which may be supported on other grounds (for instance by some trade unionists because of their fear that older workers drawing both pensions and wages will tend to depress wage levels). But it can also be justified as an indirect means test which partially, at least, achieves both the above objectives, because the people with earnings are better off than those without. Those who feel, however, that every encouragement should be given to the old to continue in employment for reasons other than simply those of finance; and those who feel that discrimination against one particular form of income, earnings, is wholly unjust when others like property income or employers' pensions are not discriminated against, will join together in advocating a more general form of income tax administered pension.

Recently, higher pensions for the old (say at 70 or 80) have been canvassed as another way of helping those who need it most, without recourse to a means test. Just how 'efficient' such a discriminatory device is depends upon the age levels adopted, the income levels it is wished to help and whether the higher pension is part of, or in place of, an overall increase.

Any indirect device, i.e. one designed to select a group for help not directly on the basis of an investigation of financial resources, but by some indirect device which it is hoped is closely associated with financial resources, is bound to be inefficient in some sense. This is an argument in favour of some income tax administered supplement to a basic pension level. The argument is that a means test administered through the completion of an income tax return which is compulsory for all, is less objectionable than the present system of national assistance. The extremely skew distribution of non-state income revealed in this survey might also lend support to the view that an income tax administered pension might bring considerable saving as compared with the cost of a substantial increase in pensions all round.[1]

A hypothetical example will illustrate this point. Let us suppose that our object is to secure an income of £5 a week for all single retirement pensioners and £8 a week for a man with a dependent wife. The cost of raising the basic pension to this level for all pensioners whilst retaining the earnings rule would be, in round figures, £480m.[2] The pension bill in the financial year ending March 1963

---

1. See Table 10.
2. This and the following calculations are based on the levels of retirement pension prevailing between May 1963 and March 1965 (see Table 4). The increase in March 1965 would affect the absolute but not the relative amount involved. It is the relative orders of magnitude which are of real interest.

was £807m. so this would be an increase of nearly 60 per cent, or 2 per cent of the national income. In absolute terms the pension bill will in any case rise over the years without any change in the pension level, as the number of pensioners increases.

An alternative way of ensuring a minimum income at the level of £5 or £8 a week might be to declare that all people qualifying on satisfaction of contribution conditions, etc., will continue to receive a pension of £3 7s. 6d. a week for a single person or £5 9s. a week for a man with a dependent wife. Those who, in addition, are willing to complete an income tax return, will be guaranteed an automatic supplement to bring the total of their income from the state up to £5 or £8 a week; except that the supplement will be reduced by the amount of one half of any income which is being received other than the basic retirement payment. Some disregard is assumed because of the view that some 'incentive' or 'reward' for self-provision is required. It would, of course, be possible to devise many variations in respect of disregards, i.e. to disregard more of certain kinds of income than of other kinds. The example taken here will assume no such discrimination, and indeed, more important, it will also assume that the special discrimination against earnings in the payment of pensions between the ages of 65 and 70 for men (60 and 65 for women) is abolished. Earnings then become a source of income like any other. An important corollary would be that the basic token payment would be made to anyone with qualifications for a pension but whose total earnings at present disbar him or her from the receipt of a pension; and it would be made in full for those whose pension is at present reduced in respect of earnings. In other words the 'earnings rule' in its present form would disappear.

Assuming that the distribution of that income which has to be taken into account in deciding how much supplement is payable is represented by the distributions in Table 10 (which gives the distribution of non-state income), it appears that the full supplement would be payable to 37 per cent of all pensioners. No supplement would be payable to single pensioners whose 'other' income exceeded £3 5s. a week; and none would be payable to couples whose 'other' income exceeded £5 2s. a week. There are, it is estimated, a quarter of all units who would receive no supplementation. The total cost of all supplementation, full and reduced, would be roughly £290m. to which approximately £90m. must be added for the token payments needed as a consequence of abolishing the earnings rule. The total cost would be £380m. or a gross saving of £90m. compared with the flat rate payment of £480m. estimated above.[1]

This is but one example of many possibilities which could be considered. The cost, for instance, of ignoring altogether the first £1 of income from other sources would be small. On an altogether grander scale, however, it might be thought desirable to make the token payment and supplementation available to all people reaching the

---

1. For details of the method of calculation of this and the other estimates and sources of the statistics used, see Appendix 3.

age of 65, irrespective of whether they had satisfied contribution conditions. This would be one way of recognising the position of those old people, mostly aged widows, who are at present excluded from pension benefit through little fault of their own. The total cost of this operation might be also of the order of £470m.; this would be made up of £290m. for existing pensioners and £180m. for old persons at present excluded from receiving a retirement pension. This suggests the rather interesting observation that one of the most costly parts of the operations considered here is the extension of the basic token payment to sections of the aged population at present excluded altogether from receiving a retirement pension.

The figures quoted are only orders of magnitude and they are figures of gross cost. A number of other factors would need to be taken into account before a precise figure could be arrived at. First, any scheme to raise pensions to these levels would, unless national assistance rates were raised pro rata, involve some saving on national assistance. How much, it would be impossible, with our present data, to say, but the total cost of weekly allowances paid by the Board to people over retirement age is at present £104m. a year.[1] To judge from the distribution of total gross income among the people receiving national assistance in our sample, the levels of income supplementation used here (£5 and £8 a week) would remove a large proportion of old people from national assistance.[2] Second, some allowance would have to be made for increased costs of administration of this sort of system, although again there would presumably be some saving on the administration of national assistance. If the levels of income guarantee discussed here are something like the ones to be considered in any real scheme, there is a very strong argument for keeping the details of the scheme as simple and straightforward as possible. At these levels of income guarantee the nature of the income distribution is such that refinements in relation to amounts or types of income to be disregarded will not make very much difference to the overall cost, but will add to administrative complexity.

Third, all the figures quoted are gross in the sense that they make no allowance for any flow back to the exchequer in the form of increased tax revenue from the higher incomes. The marginal rates of tax paid by those old people who are liable to tax must be small. But if benefits were raised to the sort of levels discussed here, either overall or by means of a supplement, there could well be a case for reviewing the present somewhat illogical system of special tax benefit for the aged with low incomes.[3] Lastly, in these calculations, no

1. Moreover the amount of saving would be affected by whether it was decided to retain some special provision for dealing with rent or other special needs. One of the objections made to an income tax administered means test is that if it is based on income alone the old person with high rent is penalised compared with his or her position under national assistance. On the other hand it is also argued that high rent payers should not be subsidised. This raises very wide issues outside the scope of this discussion. There seems no intrinsic reason, however, why the income guarantee should not be expressed in terms of a figure of total income less rent, if this is considered to be an important factor to take into account.
2. There were 10 per cent of the recipients of national assistance in the sample with total incomes above £5 for a single person and £8 for a couple, the figures with which we are working here.
3. For an interesting critical discussion of these tax concessions see Lynes, T., 'Fiscal Policy and Tax Allowances in Old Age', Paper read to the *Social Science Research Seminar of the International Gerontological Association*, Markaryd, Sweden 1963.

consideration has been given to problems of dealing with graduated additions to the retirement pension (as introduced by the National Insurance Act 1959). In the financial year 1963 expenditure on them was £130,000. Nor have we taken account of increments earned by postponing retirement. Would, for instance, accumulated rights to these benefits be preserved, and would these benefits be regarded as in the same category as, say, employers' pensions for purposes of supplementation? Questions such as these raise the fundamental issue of the contributory nature of the present national insurance scheme (as would the second of the proposals discussed on p. 131 above), and how far 'rights' are binding—an issue on which it is not proposed to comment here.

In purely monetary terms an income tax administered scheme might bring considerable savings if applied to existing pensioners alone. On the figures we quoted above it meant an expenditure of £290m. compared with £480m. for a flat rate increase. But certain consequential changes like the abolition of the earnings rule, or the extension of some supplementations to non-pensioners would reduce this saving very rapidly; and it is difficult to see just how some of these changes could be avoided. Whether or not the non-monetary price paid, i.e. of making the pension system essentially two-tier (that is, part flat-rate as of right and part income-tested), was thought to outweigh the monetary gain is a political matter. The same sort of detailed calculation could be made to illustrate the effect of, say, higher pensions at seventy. There has been no desire in this discussion to advocate one policy rather than another. Indeed, before such advocacy could begin more information would be needed about trends in future costs of the various alternatives, estimated growth of the national income, and of various other claims upon any such increase for education, investment, etc. The choice will be dictated by the priorities by which our society wishes to order its many competing claims for scarce resources. The discussion has been designed to show how the nature of such choices could be illuminated for the public much more clearly if data like those from the present survey were to be used.

The future

Whatever changes there may be in the future in the state pension scheme the data from this survey at any rate lend little support to the view that the time has come for its dismantling. Despite the fact that about 40 per cent of the men had pensions from their previous employers, the amounts they received as income from these pensions were small. While private pension rights remain largely non-transferable, interruptions in the building up of rights within schemes will tend to depress the value of benefits to be received on retirement. Moreover, there still remains a substantial proportion of people outside such private schemes. More information about coverage and the levels of benefit available in private schemes is badly needed.[1]

---

1. The survey which the Government Actuary's Department now has under way is to be welcomed.

Meantime this survey underlines once again a conclusion of the 1959/60 survey. There is a pressing need to protect or to provide adequate rights for widows in private pension schemes.

Lastly, at a time when any future pension policy seems bound to assume some form of wage-relation, it is important to remember that this survey has once again emphasised that the single largest group among the old—the single and widowed women—will always be at a disadvantage in such a framework. They are the poorest among the old today, precisely because they have not, for the most part, consistent work records; when they do work their wages are lower than those of men. The aged widow will always be with us, and no pension scheme is likely to prove satisfactory which does not recognise and meet her special needs.

CHAPTER 8

Summary and Conclusions

This is an interim report describing some of the results of a complex survey throughout Britain of persons aged 65 and over. Over 4,000 persons living in private households were interviewed during two separate periods of 1962; and information was collected during 1963 (much of it also by personal interviews) about another 2,200 living in all types of institutions except general hospitals (namely geriatric and psychiatric hospitals, nursing Homes and residential Homes).

The main object of the survey was to find how far old people are able to care for themselves, taking into account their general physical capacities, housing, income, occupations and family and social relationships.

The first part of this report is concerned with community care and starts with the use presently made of the health and welfare services by the elderly population. Approximately $4\frac{1}{2}$ per cent of persons aged 65 and over live in hospitals and other institutions. Approximately another 12 per cent are in receipt of at least one of the domiciliary health and welfare services—namely home help, meals, district nursing, chiropody, laundry and bathing (but excluding medical care).

Who are these persons? First, more of them are of advanced age and very frail. For example, 53 per cent of those in institutions and 20 per cent of those receiving domiciliary services compared with 7 per cent of the rest of the elderly population are bedfast or otherwise severely incapacitated. (A further 20 per cent, 48 per cent and 22 per cent are moderately incapacitated.) Second, rather more of them are poor and belong to the manual occupational groups. However, it must be emphasised that the middle classes (and especially the managerial and skilled non-manual groups in the population) make almost as much use of the statutory institutional and domiciliary health and welfare services as the semi-skilled and unskilled manual groups. Third, more of these old people (a) lack a family or have none within reach, or (b) have slender family resources, e.g. they depend completely on a husband or wife or an only unmarried daughter living at home.

The question of family structure is very important in understanding the reasons for institutionalisation. Far more of the old people in institutions are unmarried (33 per cent compared with 10 per cent), more lack children (26 per cent of those who are married or widowed, compared with 16 per cent), more lack brothers and sisters (40 per cent compared with 22 per cent) and more of those who have children have only one (39 per cent compared with 26 per cent) and have sons rather than daughters. Persons who have relatives but find themselves in institutions are persons who have more often led their lives in seclusion from their relatives. So in family structure and propinquity the elderly institutional population differs sharply from the rest of the population.

Those who receive health and welfare services at home also differ in family structure and propinquity from the rest of the elderly population at home. For example, 39 per cent live alone, compared with 22 per cent; 30 per cent are unmarried or childless, compared with 22 per cent; and 41 per cent do not have any relatives living within 10 minutes journey of their houses, compared with 31 per cent.

There is little evidence of health and welfare services being 'misused' or 'undermining' family responsibilities. Those who benefit from the services are mainly infirm or incapacitated persons who lack a family or have none within reach. This suggests that the family does in fact play a positive role for many old people, and a considerable body of data support this suggestion.

For example, there are over four times as many bedfast or otherwise severely incapacitated old people living at home as in all types of institutions (nearly 540,000 compared with 150,000). Most of them live with members of their families and are cared for by them, though many do not receive the supplementary social services that they (or their relatives) appear to need. However, the care provided by relatives varies in quality and more intensive inquiry into the circumstances of incapacitated old people living at home would be valuable.

Again, the evidence shows that in illness and infirmity the role of the family in providing personal and household care for the elderly dwarfs that of the social services. Of those who are ill in bed at some time in the course of a year 77 per cent, for example, rely on a spouse, children or other relatives for help with housework, 80 per cent for help with shopping and 82 per cent for help with meals, compared with 5 per cent, 2 per cent and 1 per cent who rely on the public social services.

Nonetheless, the survey also found that some services, such as district nursing and chiropody, are required by persons whether or not they can rely on the resources of the family, simply because the family is not equipped to provide such skilled professional services. This is one important fact about the respective roles of the family and the Welfare State in meeting the needs of the aged. They must increasingly be thought of as complementing each other rather than as distinct alternatives. The domiciliary services therefore perform two main positive functions. They furnish expert professional help which the family cannot supply, and they furnish unskilled or semi-skilled help for persons who do not have families and whose families living in the household or nearby are not always able or available to help.

What is the evidence of the need for an expansion of the social services? First, substantially more old people than are receiving different services feel a need and otherwise seem to qualify for them.

On the basis of the survey it can be concluded that

    (i) just over 250,000 old people depend on the local authority home help service but 330,000 feel a need for help with housework and nearly another 270,000 say they do not feel the need but have difficulty with their housework and have no one to help.

    (ii) less than 70,000 have at least one meal a week delivered by the mobile meals services and nearly another 350,000 would like to have this service.

    (iii) over 400,000 have regular chiropody treatment through a free or subsidised voluntary or local authority service but another 670,000 feel the need for someone to see to their feet regularly.

    (iv) over 200,000 have *severe* difficulties in hearing but have never had an aural examination or have not had one for more than five years.

    (v) considerable numbers have severe hearing loss but have no hearing aid or, if they have an aid, appear not to be using it regularly.

    (vi) over 300,000 have severe difficulty in seeing but have never had an examination of the eyes or have not had such an examination for more than five years.

    (vii) while the great majority of the elderly are satisfied that they see enough of their medical practitioners a minority of about 200,000 wish they saw more of them.

    (viii) only 30,000 or 40,000 are in sheltered housing (specially designed flatlets or bungalows with some community or warden services) but our evidence suggests that at least 300,000 (or 5 per cent of the elderly population) require such housing.

    (ix) over a million and half old people live in housing which lacks certain basic amenities. About 350,000 live in households which lack the sole use of a bath and of a kitchen and do not have a W.C. indoors; nearly another 1,300,000 lack two of these three basic amenities.

Second, many who are receiving certain services—particularly the hearing aid, home help and meals services—are not getting all the help they might from these services; they need help more frequently, or the service needs to be greatly improved and extended in scope.

Third, the services are poorly co-ordinated and many people receiving only one service seem to need at least two or three services. For example, 71 per cent of those having a home help have no other service; some of these feel the need for meals and chiropody services.

         *   *   *

The second part of this report is concerned with the incomes and assets of older people, and starts with a general description of the financial levels reached. On the most conservative basis it is estimated that in 1962 nearly 1¾ million men and women aged 65 and over (or about half of all single and widowed persons) had total incomes of less than £4 a week, and 400,000 couples (or just under a quarter of all couples) less than £6 per week. The median income of the women was only 16s. 6d. a week, that of the men 34s. 6d., and that of the couples 57s. 6d. above the then prevailing levels of the retirement pension. Incomes of women were less than a quarter and of couples less than a half of average industrial earnings. Median incomes were in fact about half those of comparable younger tax 'units'—i.e. single or widowed men and women, and married couples, with no dependants, who were classified as tax units by the Board of Inland Revenue. Even allowing for increases in pensions in the last three years, it can be concluded that in general the aged have income levels a half or more below the levels of younger persons in the population.

Few old people with low incomes have substantial assets. Of all income units in the 1962 survey 50 per cent of the men, 59 per cent of the women and 46 per cent of the couples had no assets or had less than £100. Comparable figures for the lowest income groups are even higher. For example, 62 per cent of women with an income of less than £2 19s. and 73 per cent of women with between £2 19s. and £3 10s. had no assets or less than £100; and these totals are each brought up to about 90 per cent if women with assets of between £100 and £500 are added. Again, little has happened in the last three years to alter the wider conclusion that a substantial section of the elderly population has very low total financial resources.

When the elderly population is considered in terms of the numbers obtaining income from different sources several important conclusions emerge. First, as many as 37 per cent (34 per cent of men, 49 per cent of women and 20 per cent of couples) are solely dependent on state benefits (predominantly retirement pensions and/or national assistance). Another 15 per cent (making 52 per cent altogether) have less than £1 a week non-state income and are therefore primarily dependent on the state.

Only 10 per cent of the women, but 21 per cent of the men and 34 per cent of the couples have employment income, some of it from part-time earnings. Elderly men's earnings are low compared with the average level of male earnings—the median income from employment of the couples in the 1962 survey being only £10 10s. (which includes some wives' earnings) and of the men £9 12s., compared with median adult male earnings of just over £15 a week in that year.

Around two-fifths of the men and of the couples but only one-tenth of the women receive pensions from employers (in the sample the figures were 36 per cent, 43 per cent and 11 per cent respectively). Half of those receiving such pensions receive them because of past employment with central and local government bodies. Many receive relatively small pensions. Nearly a quarter of the sample studied in 1962 received less than £1 a week and just under another quarter between £1 and £2 a week. There is little evidence from the survey and from other sources of private superannuation schemes providing substantial retirement incomes for a rapidly increasing proportion of the elderly population.

One important finding is that the older among the aged are certainly worse off than the younger both because of the cumulative effects of inflation on pensions but also because older people are less likely to be working. Another important finding is that women are worse off than married couples and single and widowed men in every respect. Over two-thirds are entirely or primarily dependent on the state. At all ages their median income is only about half that of couples. A considerable number of the poorest live with relatives and this may help, but many live alone. In 1962 the median weekly income of the women living alone was £3 2s.

The role of the National Assistance Board in making up the incomes of the poorest old people to a level of subsistence is extremely important. The majority of old people with national assistance have incomes above, some of them substantially above, the bare scale rates. This is explained by the Board's practice of making small discretionary additional allowances and of disregarding certain kinds and amounts of income and capital. Capital up to £125 (£375 if in war savings) is disregarded completely. But a minority live at low financial levels and yet are not in receipt of assistance. In 1962 11 per cent of the income units in the sample

(i) had total incomes of less than 5 per cent above the appropriate scale rates;
(ii) had assets of less than £100, and yet
(iii) did not receive national assistance.

They represented between 600,000 and 700,000 *individuals* in the population, compared with about 1½ million who were at that time partly or entirely dependent on national assistance. They were poor by any standards and although they cannot be regarded as all 'entitled' to assistance (because of the difficulties of interpreting the Board's standards and applying them to the survey income data), many must have been eligible.[1] Another 13 per cent, representing around ¾ million persons, also did not receive national assistance and were just above the minimum standard but still at levels of income no higher than those achieved by many who did receive national assistance.

When expenditure patterns of the elderly population are taken into account with income levels, there are grounds for concern about old people living alone. Those who live around subsistence levels are 'relatively deprived' in respect of all but a rather narrow range of conventional necessities (such as housing, food and fuel). Their expenditure on clothing, household goods and many other items is very low.

---

1. As the second edition of this report is going to press it is interesting to note that the first results of the Ministry of Pensions' own inquiry (see above p. 76) suggest that we have been unduly cautious in interpreting these figures and that in fact most of these units did have some entitlement to National Assistance. The Chancellor of the Duchy of Lancaster said in the House of Commons on 23rd February 1966 "The survey showed that there may be 700,000 retirement pensioners who would receive National Assistance if they asked for it." (*Weekly Hansard*, 18–24 February 1966, Col. 431).

The implications of all these findings for policies in social security are that attention needs urgently to be given to the problem of the aged widows, to the older groups among the aged, to the gulf which exists financially between the 10 per cent who continue to work full-time and those of the elderly who are retired, and, finally, to the marked difference in income levels between a majority of the elderly and younger persons—even those living in comparable circumstances, such as younger single and widowed persons and childless married couples living on their own.

Appendix 1—Social Surveys of Old People 1945-64

SELECTED LIST

Date of Survey	Area	Numbers interviewed	References
1945-46 (?)	Lutterworth, Midhurst, Mid-Rhondda, Wolverhampton, Oldham, Wandsworth and St. Pancras	2,302 people of pensionable age	Nuffield Foundation, Survey Committee on the Problems of Ageing and the Care of Old People (1947), *Old People*, London, Oxford University Press
1945-7	Wolverhampton	477 people of pensionable age	Sheldon, J. H. (1948), *The Social Medicine of Old Age; Report of an Inquiry in Wolverhampton*, London, Oxford University Press
1948	Sheffield	1,596 people of pensionable age	Greenlees, A. and Adams, J. (1950), *Old People in Sheffield*, Sheffield
1948	Birmingham	2,230 people over 70	Shenfield, B. E. (1957), *Social Policies for Old Age*, London
1949-50	Plymouth	Chiefly 80 housebound on list of 350 kept by home help service	Plymouth Council of Social Service (1950), *Housebound*, Plymouth
1949-51	Sheffield	476 living alone or with spouse (mainly health but also social)	Hobson, W. and Pemberton, J. (1955), *The Health of the Elderly at Home*, London; see also Bransby, E. R. and Osborne, B. (1953), *British Journal of Nutrition*, 7, 160. Osborne, B. (1951), *The Nutrition of Older People* (unpublished report of a government social survey)
1950	Northern Ireland	759 people aged 60 and over	Adams, C. F. and Cheeseman, E. A. (1951), *Old People in Northern Ireland. A Report to the Northern Ireland Hospitals Authority*, Belfast

Date of Survey	Area	Numbers interviewed	References
1950	Great Britain	1,950 men and 482 women aged 55–74	Thomas, G. and Osborne, B. (1950), *Older People and Their Employment* (Social survey for Ministry of Labour and National Services. Report No. 150/1—and unpublished). Summarized by Moss, L. (1955), A sample survey of older people and their employment in Great Britain in 1950. In: *Old Age in the Modern World* (Report of the Third Congress of the International Association of Gerontology, London, 1954). Edinburgh, Livingstone, p. 353
1951	Lewisham and Camberwell	1,082 households with at least one person over 65 being helped by domestic help and/or district nursing service	Chalke, H. D. and Benjamin. B. (1953), *Lancet.* 1, 588
1951–52	Liverpool	500 people of pensionable age in 5 selected districts	Liverpool Personal Service Society and Liverpool University, Department of Social Science (1953), *Social Contacts in Old Age*, Liverpool
1953	Hammersmith	100 people over 70 living alone	Sir Halley Stewart Trust and National Old People's Welfare Committee (1954), *Over Seventy*, National Council of Social Service, London
1954	Edinburgh	2,768 people aged 60 and over	Gordon, C.; Thompson, J. G. and Emerson, A. R. (1957), *Medical Officer*, 98, 19
1954	Great Britain	120,000 people receiving assistance aged 80 years and over and living alone	Great Britain, National Assistance Board (1955), *Report for the year ended 31 December*, 1954, London, H.M. Stationery Office
1954–55	Rutherglen	323 men aged 65 and over	Anderson, W. F. and Cowan, N. R. (1955), *Lancet*, 2, 239
1954–55	Bethnal Green	203 people of pensionable age	Townsend, P. (1957), *The Family Life of Old People; an Inquiry in East London*, London, Routledge & Kegan Paul
1955	Aberdeen	244 retired men aged 65–74	Richardson, I. M. (1956), *Scottish Medical Journal*, 1, 381

Date of Survey	Area	Numbers interviewed	References
1955	Nottinghamshire (two areas)	340 people aged 65 and over	Marsh, D. C. (1955), *Elderly People*, Nottingham
1955	Dundee	400 people aged 65 and over	Mair, A., Weir, I. B. L. and Wilson, W. A. (1955), *Public Health (London)*, 70, 97
1956–57	Stockport	2,073 people aged 80 and over	Lempert, S. (1958), *Report on the Survey of the Aged in Stockport*, Stockport, County Borough of Stockport
1957	Anglesey	160 persons aged 65 and over	Wynne Griffith, G., *The Needs of Old People in Rural Areas* (Paper read to the Royal Society of Health Congress, Eastbourne, 1958), *Journal of the Royal Society for the Promotion of Health*, July/August 1958
1957	Orkney	233 people of pensionable age	Richardson, I. M., Brodie, A. S. and Wilson, S. (1959), 'Social and Medical Needs of Old People in Orkney: Report of a Social Survey', *Health Bulletin, Scotland*, Vol. 17, No. 4
1957	Woodford	210 persons of pensionable age	Willmott, P., and Young, M. (1960), *Family and Class in a London Suburb*, London, Routledge & Kegan Paul
1958–60	Aberdeen	474 people aged 60 and over	Richardson, I. M. (1964), *Age and Need*, E. and S. Livingstone, Edinburgh
1958	Great Britain	853 people receiving meals in areas with a meals service; 1,317 people of pensionable age living in private households	Harris, A. I., *Meals on Wheels for Old People: A Report of an Inquiry by the Government Social Survey*, London, The National Corporation for the Care of Old People, 1960
1958–59	Rural area in Shropshire	328 people of pensionable age	Miller, M. C. (1963), *The Ageing Countryman: A Socio-Medical Report on Old Age in a Country Practice*, London, National Corporation for the Care of Old People
1958–60	England and Wales	489 residents of Homes and Institutions who were of pensionable age (other information also about 8,000 persons of pensionable age	Townsend, P. (1962), *The Last Refuge: A Survey of Residential Institutions and Homes for the Aged in England and Wales*, London, Routledge & Kegan Paul

Date of Survey	Area	Numbers interviewed	References
1959–60	Seven Areas: Salisbury, Leicester, Hexham Rural District, Seaton Valley, Glasgow, Wimbledon and East Ham	1,078 'units' consisting of one person or a married couple of pensionable age	Cole Wedderburn, D., with Utting, J. (1962), *The Economic Circumstances of Old People*, Occasional Papers on Social Administration, No. 4, Welwyn, Herts, The Codicote Press
1960	Lewisham	1,370 people aged 65 and over	Harris, A. I. assisted by Woolf, M., *Health and Welfare of Older People in Lewisham*, The Social Survey, Central Office of Information, June 1962
1960	Swansea	1,962 individuals of all ages, including about 200 aged 65 and over	(Preliminary) Rosser, C. and Harris, C. C. (1961), 'Relationships through Marriage in a Welsh Urban Area', *The Sociological Review*, Vol. 9, No. 3, pp. 293–321
1960–61	Newcastle-upon-Tyne	123 people aged 65 and over in geriatric wards of hospitals and in Residential Homes (together with other information)	Kay, D. W. K., Beamish, P. and Roth, M. (1962), 'Some Medical and Social Characteristics of Elderly People under State Care' in Halmos, P. (ed.), *The Sociological Review*, Monograph, No. 5
1962	Barrow	829 old people living at home (and other information about elderly hospital patients)	Edge, J. R. and Nelson, I. D. M. (1963 and 1964), 'Survey of Arrangements for the Elderly in Barrow-in-Furness. 1 and 2', *Medical Care*, 1964, Vol. 2, No. 1, p. 7
1962	West Hartlepool	320 people aged 75 and over living alone	Bamlett, R. and Milligan, H. C. (1963), 'Health and Welfare Services and the Over 75's', *The Medical Officer*, CIX No. 25
1962–63	Edinburgh	200 people aged 65 and over	Williamson, J., *et al.*, 'Old People at Home: Their Unreported Needs' (May 25th, 1964), *The Lancet*

Appendix 2—Sample Design and Sampling Error

(Compiled with the generous help of Mr. Ronald Blunden of the Government Social Survey)

Sample design

The population, from which a representative sample was to be selected with known probability, was defined as persons aged 65 years and over living in private households in England, Wales and Scotland.

The sample design was a stratified multi-stage one in three stages with local authority administrative areas as the primary sampling units. These primary units of which there are about 2,000 were grouped into the 11 standard regions as defined by the Registrar-General. Scotland, one of the regions, was further sub-divided into the four divisions: Northern (including the Crofting Counties)—East Central, West Central and Southern. Within these strata, primary units were further stratified into conurbations where these existed, other urban units outside the conurbations and rural units. The conurbations are primarily composed of high population-density county boroughs, municipal boroughs and urban districts in England, with two high-density rural areas, Elstree R.D. and Disley R.D., being included; in Scotland the Clydeside conurbation consists of high-density burghs and the high-density district council areas surrounding Glasgow. The remaining county boroughs, municipal boroughs and urban districts in England and Wales and the large and small burghs in Scotland comprised the other urban stratum. Other rural districts in England and Wales and district council areas in Scotland formed the rural stratum. In England and Wales, within each of these strata primary units were further stratified by the J-index, i.e. the proportion of the population of an area liable for jury service, which was used as an index of the economic status of an area. Qualification for jury service being different in Scotland, the rateable value per head of population was used as a stratifying factor. The frame having been formed in this manner, 80 primary sampling units were selected with probability proportionate to their parliamentary electorate. The further stages of sampling for both phases of interviewing were undertaken in these same primary units.

At the second stage of sampling, addresses were selected with unit probability from the electoral registers for the selected primary units. Previous evidence had indicated that, on average, one in every three private addresses in the register contained older persons as defined, and that at each address in which these older persons lived, there were on average approximately 1·3 such persons. At each address in the sample which contained persons aged 65 years and over, all such persons were to be included in the sample. Approximately 8,000 addresses were selected for the first phase and 5,000 for the second,

144

the overall probability of selection of addresses in either phase being uniform. From the units selected it was expected that a sample of about 4,000 persons aged 65 years and over would be obtained from a population of approximately 6,207,000.

Estimates

The estimates in this report have been derived from the data collected at the time of interview with no adjustment being made for the unproductive element of the sample.

Reliability of estimates

The estimates given in this report are those based on the results obtained from a sample of the male and female population of England, Wales and Scotland, aged 65 years and over, selected by using a stratified multi-stage sample design. As in all sample surveys the results are subject to various forms of error. Some error will arise due to sampling variability and is calculable; other error may arise through the various forms of non-response of some of the sample. This non-response can be due to such factors as the interviewer being unable to make contact with the person during the field period, either because he or she is always out or away on holiday: or the person may be too ill or incapacitated to be interviewed although still at home, or the person may just refuse to co-operate. The effects of this non-response on the estimates are not known. The standard error is hence primarily a measure on the sampling variability, that is, of the variations which arise by chance through taking only a sample and not the whole population, and does not measure the error or bias arising from non-response. It can be stated with 68 per cent confidence that an estimate obtained from the sample will differ from an actual population figure by less than ± one standard error and with 95 per cent confidence that the difference will be less than ± twice the standard error.

Sampling variance of the estimates

In multi-stage stratified probability sampling approximate figures for the variance on the estimates attributable to sampling can be estimated from the variable in the selected primary sampling units without considering the variation within a primary sampling unit. It requires that two or more primary units are selected from each stratum and an estimate of the contribution from each stratum can then be made directly from the variance between the selected primary units in the stratum. The assumption made is that primary units are drawn with replacement and the final units selected with a uniform overall sampling ratio. The variance of a mean may then be estimated as:

$$\text{Var}\bar{x} = \frac{1}{n^2} \sum \frac{m_i}{m_i - 1} (X_{ij} - \overline{X}_i)^2$$

where n is the number of final units in the sample.

145

X_{ij} is the aggregate value of x obtained from the jth primary unit in the ith stratum.

$\overline{X}_i$ is the mean of the m_i primary units selected from the ith stratum.

In practice this formula needs to be modified to allow for failure to achieve 100 per cent co-operation and in particular it becomes necessary to re-define the aggregate values. However, as it is unlikely that any great error is involved in using the single-stage random sampling formula, the approximations to the standard errors of the estimates have been calculated on this basis. The three tables below show the standard error for both sample percentages and population estimates based on the results of the survey. In considering them in relation to figures in the text the reader should remember that we have been able to compare a number of the figures produced by the survey with independent national data (e.g. the numbers receiving the home help and meals services and the numbers seeing a doctor during a year). These figures have corresponded closely.

TABLE 1

Standard errors of estimates of numbers of persons aged 65 years and over based on sample of approximately 4,000

(68 per cent confidence limits)

Size of estimate (000s)	Approximate standard error (000s)
50	8·4
100	12·0
200	15·5
500	26·0
1,000	35·0
2,000	45·9
3,000	47·4

TABLE 2

Standard error of estimated percentages of persons aged 65 years and over based on a sample of approximately 4,000

(68 per cent confidence limits)

Estimated percentage	Standard error %
2 or 98	0·22
5 or 95	0·34
10 or 90	0·47
25 or 75	0·68
50	0·79

146

TABLE 3

Standard error of estimated percentages based upon various sample sizes
(68 per cent confidence limits)

Estimated percentage			Sample size (base of percentage)												
			100	250	500	750	1,000	1,500	2,000	2,500	3,000	3,500	4,000
2 or 98	.	...	±1·40	±0·89	±0·63	±0·51	±0·44	±0·36	±0·31	±0·28	±0·26	±0·24	±0·22
5 or 95	.	...	±2·18	±1·38	±0·97	±0·80	±0·70	±0·56	±0·49	±0·44	±0·40	±0·37	±0·34
10 or 90	.	...	±3·00	±1·90	±1·34	±1·09	±0·95	±0·77	±0·67	±0·60	±0·55	±0·51	±0·47
25 or 75	..	...	±4·33	±2·74	±1·94	±1·58	±1·37	±1·11	±0·97	±0·87	±0·79	±0·73	±0·68
50	...	...	±5·00	±3·33	±2·24	±1·83	±1·58	±1·29	±1·12	±1·00	±0·91	±0·85	±0·79

Appendix 3—Method of calculating cost of various schemes for increasing the Retirement Pension

(see pp. 129–131 of text)

Sources

1. *Annual Report of Ministry of Pensions and National Insurance*— 1963 (Cmnd. 2392) which gives:

 (a) Numbers of Retirement Pensions in payment in the following categories

 Men
 Wives on husband's insurance
 Women on own insurance ⎫ by age
 Widows on husband's insurance ⎭

 (b) Number of people deferring retirement.
 (c) Widows' benefit—payment to widows aged 60–64.

2. *Economic Trends*, Sept. 1962, which gives the estimate of percentage of women 60 and over who are single, widowed, etc.

3. Ministry of Pensions and National Insurance, *Abstract of Statistics* 1961, which gives the number of women 60+ married to men under 65. This has been increased by the percentage increase in the number of women 60 and over between 1961 and 1963.

(1) *Estimate of number of income units among existing retirement pensioners*

 (a) Assume 70 per cent of all men receiving pensions are married (1959–60 Survey showed 69·3 per cent of men 65+ were married; the 1962 national survey showed 71 per cent 65+ were married).

 This gives the total number of couple retirement pensioner income units and the number of single men:

 1,397,000 couples
 599,000 men

 (b) Deduct number of wives receiving pension on husband's insurance from total number of couples to give number of wives receiving pension in own right, that is 304,000. This is probably an overestimate since some men 65+ may be married to women still working and not drawing a pension.

 (c) Then women on own insurance less wives in own right as above (1,584,000 minus 304,000) plus widows on husband's insurance, 1,323,000 plus 157,000 widow pensioners aged 60

148

and over gives the total number of single or widowed women income units:

2,760,000 women

(2) *Estimate of number of income units among existing pensioners and those who have deferred retirement.*

(a) As above.

(b) Of the 280,000 men deferring retirement, assume 70 per cent married and add to (a):

1,593,000 couples
683,000 men

(c) To calculate number of wives, assume thirty per cent of the women deferring retirement are married; then a total of 340,000 wives will have pension in own right. Thus 1,379,000 women with pensions in their own right together with 1,323,000 widows with pension on husband's insurance and 157,000 widow pensioners gives the total number of women income units:

2,860,000 women

(3) *Estimate of numbers of income units in the population over 60/65 including only couples where the man is 65+ irrespective of wife's age*

(a) Total population aged 60+ women and 65+ men in Great Britain, June 1963

5,393,000 women
2,358,000 men

(b) Assume 70 per cent of men are married then income units who are couples number 1,651,000; and single or widowed men number 707,000.

(c) There were 3,145,000 women aged 60+ who were single or widowed.

(4) *Summary of various estimates (rounded) of numbers of income units*

	A Existing retirement pensioners	B Retirement pensioners plus men and women deferring retirement	C All men and women over 60/65: (i) excluding women 60+ married to men aged under 65 (ii) and including women under 60 married to men 65+
	Thousands	Thousands	Thousands
Men	599	680	710
Women	2,800	2,900	3,100
Couples	1,400	1,600	1,650

149

(5) *Method of calculating cost of increasing pensions in various ways:*

(1) *Flat rate increase to all retirement pensioners.* The amount of the weekly increase has been multiplied by the actual numbers in the various categories of pensioner at December 1963.

(2) *Income tax administered supplement* involves two stages of calculation:

    (i) First estimate the cost of paying the flat-rate token payment to all income units in categories B and C above who are not now receiving retirement pensions.

    (ii) Estimate the number of income units who would receive varying amount of supplement by applying the percentages of units with varying amounts of non-state income from a more detailed version of Table 10 of the text to the estimates in B and C above. Assume all units in each interval to be receiving the mid-point non-state income of that interval. The supplement payable to each unit in that interval is then the full supplement payable, minus the mid-point income.